Exploring Delmarva

■ ■ ■

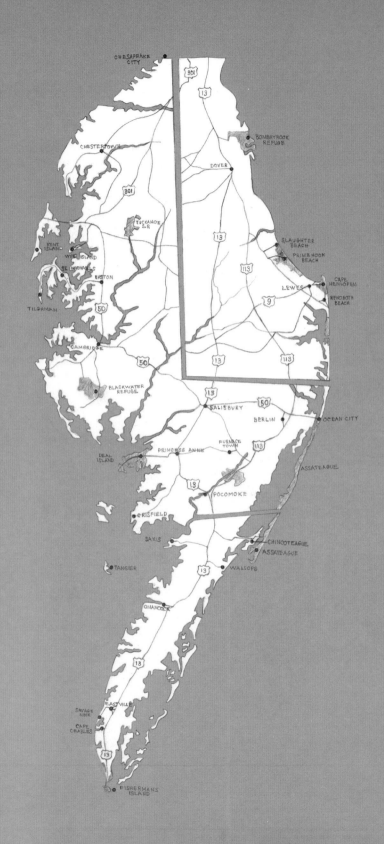

Exploring Delmarva

A Travel Guide from Cape Charles

to Chesapeake City

Curtis J. Badger

■ ■ ■

CORNELL MARITIME PRESS

A Division of Schiffer Publishing Ltd.

Atglen Pennsylvania

Other Schiffer Books by the Author:
Making Decoys: The Century Old Way, 978-0-87033-579-2, $24.95

Designed by RoS
Type set in Garamond Premier Pro

ISBN: 978-0-87033-633-1
Printed in China

Published by Schiffer Publishing, Ltd.
4880 Lower Valley Road
Atglen, PA 19310
Phone: (610) 593-1777; Fax: (610) 593-2002
E-mail: Info@schifferbooks.com

For our complete selection of fine books on this and related subjects, please visit our website at www.schifferbooks.com. You may also write for a free catalog.

This book may be purchased from the publisher. Please try your bookstore first.

We are always looking for people to write books on new and related subjects. If you have an idea for a book, please contact us at proposals@schifferbooks.com.

Schiffer Publishing's titles are available at special discounts for bulk purchases for sales promotions or premiums. Special editions, including personalized covers, corporate imprints, and excerpts can be created in large quantities for special needs. For more information, contact the publisher.

Book illustrations were done by Mary Ann Clarke.

Dedication

*To my wife, Lynn, and son, Tom, who shared many
of these trips with me, and made the experience
that much more special.*

and

*To the reader, may your family also share
our joy in discovering these places that make
Delmarva special.*

Contents

Preface

Many years ago, Scorchy Tawes, the beloved outdoors reporter for WBOC-TV in Salisbury, made a promo for his show with Franc White, host of *The Southern Sportsman*. "I come to Delmarva every chance I get," said Franc.

"And I stay here every chance I get," replied Scorchy.

At that time, I was something of a young and callow lad, bitten by the adventure bug, and I couldn't understand why anyone would want to stay on Delmarva when there was a wide and wonderful world to explore. I'd look at a map of the Yorkshire Dales and dream of exploring villages with names such as "Giggleswick" and "Appletreewick." I'd read about Mayan ruins in Mexico and began squirreling away my dollars for a trip.

In the interim, I've been to the Yorkshire Dales. Our family had a memorably cold March hike along the Pennine Way at Malham Beck. We walked the streets of London. We drove to Lands End. We went to Chichen Itza, Tulum, and Xel Ha in the Yucatan. We ate broiled fish on the beach of Isla de Mujeres.

And now, finally, I'm beginning to understand Scorchy. I don't want to do that anymore. I want to stay on Delmarva every chance I get.

Here are some things I don't want to do anymore:

- I don't want to wait in airports for hours.
- I don't want to have to take my shoes off and get patted down to get on an airplane.
- I don't want to have my toothpaste confiscated.
- I don't want to worry about missing connecting flights or getting bumped from the one I bought a ticket for.
- I don't want to eat bad food from plastic containers with my elbows pinned to my sides.

- I don't want the passenger in front of me tilting his seat back until his head is in my lap for the duration of an eight-hour flight.
- I don't want to go bleary-eyed through customs and get questioned by some starched uniform with an attitude.
- I don't want to stay in overpriced hotel rooms with uncomfortable beds.
- I don't want to eat bland twenty-dollar hamburgers.
- I don't want to drink warm beer.
- I don't want to have my Coke without ice.

I've spent the last year of my life exploring Delmarva, and I can honestly say I don't want to go anywhere else. From where I live on the Virginia portion of the peninsula, I can take a leisurely drive and spend a long weekend visiting wonderful places and meeting people with whom I feel a deep kinship. The fifty adventures described here are just the tip of the iceberg, just the beginning. There are extraordinary places to discover down back roads on Delmarva, creeks to paddle, fish to catch, wonderful food to eat...a world of discovery to be found here in the three states that make up our peninsula. I think my sense of adventure, my love of travel, is still intact. I've just learned to focus it closer to home, to enjoy the things around me.

In the past year, I've come to realize that those of us who live on Delmarva enjoy a special kinship. I've always considered myself a Virginian; my tax dollars go to Richmond, I vote for state officials, and I was indoctrinated in Virginia history in grade school, but I realize now that the culture that has shaped my life and my values has much more in common with Delmarva, rather than the portion of Virginia that lies west of the Chesapeake Bay. While I dearly love Virginia, I suspect my connection to the Commonwealth is more political than cultural, more legal than personal.

For a moment, let's forget about the geopolitical boundaries — the state lines — that separate the three states that make up the Delmarva Peninsula. Suddenly, we have much in common. We live in a mostly rural environment. Our history and culture are tied to the land, and certainly to the water that surrounds us. We hunt and fish, we farm and raise corn and tomatoes in our gardens. We go clamming and crabbing. We enjoy being on the water and hate to contemplate life away from it.

We even gather and prepare our food in a similar manner. For example, you could go anywhere on Delmarva — from Rock Hall to Cape Charles — and ask someone the best way to cook spot — and you would get the same answer. Spot should be fried, never broiled or baked, and certainly never poached. Purists will tell you the head and tail should be left on. Purists of a certain age will tell you the head and tail should be left on and the spot should be fried in bacon drippings.

Now, head west, go one hundred miles inland, and ask someone the best way to cook spot. You're likely to be arrested, handcuffed, and taken away, charged with having culinary intent toward the family dog.

As I previously pointed out, Delmarva consists of portions of the three states (**DEL**aware, **MA**ryland, and Virgini**A**) that make up the peninsula that separates the Chesapeake Bay from the Atlantic Ocean, Delaware Bay, and Delaware River. The eastern, western, and southern boundaries are easily defined. The northern boundary can be open to speculation. For the purposes of this book, I have used the Chesapeake and Delaware Canal as the boundary. On the map, this line makes a handy divider. I extend my sincere apologies to anyone who lives north of the canal who may feel slighted or excluded, but we have to draw a line somewhere and I think the canal defines certain cultural, as well as geographical, differences. Cross the canal and head north to Newark, Wilmington, and Philadelphia, and you're definitely in an urban setting. Drive along the I-95 corridor and you can be sure you are no longer on Delmarva.

Whether you are a visitor to our peninsula or a full-time resident, I hope these fifty adventures will open your eyes to the wealth of places we have to explore and experience and, unlike most of modern travel, getting there is part of the fun. It has been a delightful project for me, one that, perhaps belatedly, has opened my eyes to the treasures we have here on Delmarva. I plan to stay here every chance I get.

Acknowledgments

This book would not be possible without the advice, encouragement, and generosity of many people who have a special kinship with Delmarva. I'm especially indebted to so many folks who took the time to show me places on our peninsula that I would not have found on my own. Special thanks go to an old newspaper colleague, Cindy Small, of Kent County, Delaware, and her husband David.

Thanks also go to Michelle Robinette and Nate Davidson of Kent County; Tina Watson of Bombay Hook National Wildlife Refuge; Mike Leister of the Air Force AMC Museum; Dawn Webb of the DuPont Nature Center; Jim O'Neill of Delaware State Parks; Bernadette Van Pelt of the Kent County Maryland tourism office; Capt. Mark and Suzanne Einstein of Rock Hall; Barbara Siegert and Judy Edelheit of the Queen Anne's County tourism office; Nancy Cook of the Kent Island Heritage Society; Ellie Altman of the Adkins Arboretum; Capt. Buddy Harrison of the Chesapeake House at Tilghman Island; Sandy Fulton of Wicomico County Tourism; Lora Bottinelli of the Ward Museum at Salisbury University; Lisa Challenger of the Worcester County Tourism Commission; Jim Rapp of Delmarva Low Impact Tourism Experiences; Joe Fehrer of The Nature Conservancy's Nassawango Preserve; Kathy Fisher of Furnace Town; Jim Bellas of Bike to Go in Rehoboth; Deanna Hickman of the NASA Wallops Visitor Center; Dot Field of the Virginia Department of Conservation and Recreation Division of Natural Heritage; Jethro Runco of the Coastal Virginia Wildlife Observatory at Kiptopeke; Jenny and George Budd of Fisherman Island National Wildlife Refuge; and Laura Vaughan and Jerry Doughty of the Eastern Shore of Virginia Barrier Islands Center.

Again, thanks so much, all of you.

Introduction

The Best of Delmarva

If you spend a lot of time exploring Delmarva, you soon discover favorite places and activities, and you come across some locations that surprise you. Herewith is a very personal and totally un-objective list of some of my Delmarva favorites.

BEST BACK ROADS: The winner is the state of Maryland, which consistently has wide, smooth, well-paved, litter-free, secondary roads. These roads are bicycle-friendly and make visitors feel welcome. State Routes 213 and 313, for example, are wonderful north-south alternatives to the more congested, well-traveled highways. You will especially appreciate Maryland's back roads when leaving the state and entering either of the other two that make up Delmarva.

BEST PLACE TO BRING AN APPETITE: The waterfront town of Onancock, Virginia. For a town of only 1,500 people, Onancock has some wonderful small restaurants, offering everything from fresh local seafood to European cuisine. There also are natural food shops, a farmers' market, a store specializing in gourmet cookware, and a wine bar.

BEST PUBLIC CAMPGROUND: Pocomoke River State Park at Shad Landing, near Snow Hill. The campsites are spacious, and all are in groves of huge pines and hardwoods. The river runs through the park, and there are naturalist programs on a regular basis. The facilities include a swimming pool, fishing pond, walking trail, playgrounds, group picnic area, nature center, cabins, and a camp store. You can fall asleep to the sounds of pileated woodpeckers.

BEST PLACE TO TAKE A HIKE: Adkins Arboretum near Ridgely, Maryland. There are birds, butterflies, gardens of native plants, and a trail that winds through a bottomland hardwood forest. What makes it special is that the arboretum regularly has displays of environmental art placed along the trail, often in surprising locations.

BEST PLACE TO PADDLE: This is a toss-up between the upper Pocomoke River and Nassawango Creek in Maryland. Put in at Porter's Crossing on the Pocomoke or Red House Road on the Nassawango and enjoy a six-mile paddle to Snow Hill.

BEST SURPRISE: Chesapeake City, Maryland, on the C&D Canal. A historic town nicely restored, without feeling like a restored historic town.

BEST PLACE TO SHOP FOR ANTIQUES: Four-way tie: Lewes and Millsboro in Delaware; Berlin and Galena in Maryland.

BEST PLACE TO GET FRESH MUSKRATS: Susan's Seafood in New Church, Virginia, and Morris' Market in Frederica, Delaware, which also advertises fresh coon meat and Hughes scrapple, a Delmarva delicacy made in nearby Felton. Some folks don't like scrapple. I think of it as pig paté.

BEST PLACE TO BUY PORK PRODUCTS: Forget about Walmart and Food Lion. Find a mom and pop store in a small town in Delaware. The best are sure to have the aforementioned Hughes scrapple, as well as Milton sausage, wonderfully lean and spicy and made right here in Harrington.

BEST ROAD SIGN: On a country store in Wenona, west of Deal Island: "This ain't the end of the world, but you can see it from here."

BEST SMALL MUSEUM: The Air Mobility Command Museum in Dover. I know. The name is a little off-putting, as though you were expected to stand at attention for the duration of your visit, but this is a great place to explore and by all means bring the kids. They can climb aboard vintage aircraft, try their hand at a flight simulator, and learn about Delmarva's role in World War II. Many exhibits are in a huge, historic hangar, and many more are outside. Plus, admission is free.

Best Large Museum: The Chesapeake Bay Maritime Museum in St. Michaels. It's a wonderful place that keeps getting better.

Best Room with a View: If your idea of a great view is a sunrise over an open ocean, book a room in one of the high-rise hotels in Ocean City. In the winter, the views are great and the rates are a bargain. If NASCAR and harness racing are more to your taste, check out Dover Downs and get a room overlooking the track.

Best Place to see Birds: Kiptopeke State Park in Virginia near the southern tip of the Delmarva Peninsula. Birds gather here in great numbers before crossing the Chesapeake on their way to winter homes in Central and South America.

Best Place to Play Golf: Northern region: Ocean City area. Southern Region: Bay Creek Resort at Cape Charles.

Best Place to Fish: The barrier islands of Virginia. They are remote and have no facilities at all. If you can handle a wilderness experience, it's worth the trip, whether or not you catch fish.

Best Unspoiled Natural Area: See above.

Best Place to Ride a Bike (short trip): Chincoteague National Wildlife Refuge. The refuge has about ten miles of biking/hiking trails. In the fall and winter you ride among flocks of thousands of waterfowl, not to mention Chincoteague ponies...not flocks, but herds.

Best Ride (long trip): Pick a back road in Maryland, any back road.

Best Ride on a Windy Day: Trap Pond State Park near Laurel, Delaware. More than five miles of trails wind their way through pine and hardwood forest and bottomland swamp. Most of the trail is sheltered the entire way, so the wind is seldom a factor.

Best Surprise Bike Ride: The Boardwalk in Ocean City. In the summer, you're cheek-to-jowl with tourists, but go on a mild day in the winter, preferably mid-week, and you'll have a ride of about five miles with the ocean on one side and the wonderful old clapboard Ocean City hotels and attractions on the other.

Now, here are a few personal preferences and opinions, gained from many months of hiking, biking, and boating around Delmarva.

Best Snack Food For a Hike: An orange and a chunk of dark chocolate.

Best Hiking Accessory I Thought I'd Never Want: A walking stick. I used to use a sassafras sapling that honeysuckle had wound around, creating a great spiral pattern. I peeled off the bark, varnished the wood, and used it as a walking stick. Frankly, it was more an affectation than a functional accessory. It was heavy and brittle, and if I were to trip, I had little confidence it would support my weight.

After Lynn and I both had knee surgery a few years ago, we bought a pair of super lightweight Leki metal walking sticks made in Czechoslovakia. We each use one. The sticks are adjustable, weigh next to nothing, have spring-loaded tips to soften impact, and are very strong. They are not inexpensive, but if they prevent just one twisted ankle or sprained knee, the price was a bargain.

Tips for Making Your Visits Better

Dress Well: Hiking shoes, clothes, and accessories are available at great prices at discount stores, but if you plan to use your equipment a lot, it pays to invest in the highest quality available, especially when it comes to shoes and clothing. Good quality equipment provides comfort and lasts far longer than discount merchandise. Buy from dealers who specialize in outdoor equipment and whose staff are familiar with the goods, whether it's hiking boots, trail clothing, backpacks, bikes, or canoes.

Respect Others: When we hike, bike, or canoe on Delmarva, chances are we'll be enjoying public lands and waters. If you leave trash behind, you'll diminish the outdoor experience for those who come after you. If you're riding a bike on a multiple-use trail, let hikers know you're approaching if coming from behind. If hikers have stopped to watch birds or other wildlife, stop and let them have their quiet moments.

Volunteer: Most of the public areas you'll explore on Delmarva, whether wildlife refuges or state natural areas, depend heavily on volunteers. They man visitor centers, maintain trails, lead birding trips, pick up trash, help with research, and perform countless other tasks. Try it yourself. Pick a park or refuge near your home, contact the volunteer coordinator, and join the volunteer team. It will be one of the most rewarding experiences of your outdoor life.

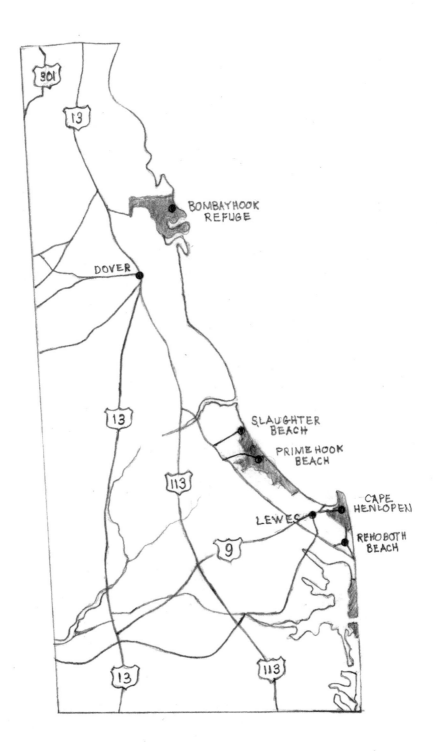

301

13

BOMBAY HOOK
REFUGE

DOVER

13

SLAUGHTER
BEACH

PRIME HOOK
BEACH

113

CAPE
HENLOPEN

LEWES

REHOBOTH
BEACH

9

13

113

DELAWARE

Delaware Adventures

■ ■ ■

Delaware is what you could call a compact state. It's not large, but there is a lot going on in a fairly concentrated area. For example, the old part of Dover is rich in history and culture. The city has two state capital buildings, the oldest dating back to 1792. It was the first state to ratify the Constitution, which was signed on The Green in 1787. So if it's history you want, downtown Dover is the place to go.

If you're looking for a little more glitter, though, a short drive north will take you to Dover Downs, one of the fastest-growing convention centers in the state. There are the slots, the entertainers, and, of course, NASCAR racing. Also, shopping malls abound just next door.

Let's say your interests run more toward the outdoors and nature. Within minutes you can be tooling through farmland and salt marshes on Route 9, passing through quiet towns such as Leipsic, heading toward Bombay Hook National Wildlife Refuge and its thousands of acres of protected land. In the winter, there will be snow geese by the tens of thousands, huge flocks so thick that they appear to be clouds shifting along the horizon.

Our Delaware trips emphasize strongly the First State's coastline, reflecting both human history and natural history. Refuges, such as Bombay Hook and, farther south, Prime Hook, include miles and miles of wild coast and salt marsh meadows stretching as far as the eye can see and towns, such as Lewes, founded as a Dutch whaling center, capture the seafaring spirit of the Delaware coast.

The Rehoboth area is a popular beach resort, complete with boardwalk and saltwater taffy. Nearby, Cape Henlopen State Park offers camping, the beach, and hundreds of acres of dunes to explore.

As you will see, Delaware offers something for all interests and all tastes, from the thrill of the gaming table to quiet walks in pristine coastal wilderness or a day at the beach. Delaware is not a large state, but it is Delmarva's most diverse.

1

Dover

A Capital Idea

Let's say the three states that make up Delmarva decided to band together and form a commonwealth of their own, the 51st state of the union. After all, it's not such a far-fetched idea. Remove the current state lines and you'll find a peninsula with people who have a great deal in common. Our economy is based on agriculture and tourism, we have a great fondness for bays and the ocean, and we have a similar culture. Travel north and south on Delmarva and you'll find communities that have a certain kinship; head west, across the Chesapeake, and you're in a different world, no matter what state you're in.

If this were to happen — if we were to create the state of Delmarva — we would need a capital. I humbly nominate Dover. Now, here is a city that knows a thing or two about governance. Dover has been a capital city since 1777, and it comes with not one but two capitol buildings. The Old State House was built in 1792 and the more recent Legislative Hall became the seat of state government in 1933. Dover is the only state capital on Delmarva.

There really are two Dovers: one sleek and modern and ready for anything; the other traditional, historic, and laid back. The first Dover is sandwiched between Route 13 and the Route 1 bypass. Here we have Dover Downs with its glittering casinos and convention center, the speedway, harness racing, restaurants, shopping malls, and, west of Route 13, the campus of Delaware State University, which seems to be constantly expanding with new facilities.

The traditional Dover is in the downtown historic area, home of the famous Green, the statehouses, taverns, churches, historic cemeteries, shops, galleries, and museums. In contrast to the modern Dover, this Dover is more quiet and reflective, attuned to its place in the history of the First State, a name bestowed upon Delaware because in 1787 its delegates were the first to ratify the United States Constitution. They signed the document at the Golden Fleece Tavern on Dover's public square, which later became known as The Green, just up the street from the State House.

Dover places great value on its place in history and has created the First State Heritage Park, something of an umbrella organization that encompasses many of the historic buildings and programs associated with the historic district. "It's something like Colonial Williamsburg, but it didn't have to be re-created," said Michele Robinette of the Kent County Convention and Visitors Bureau. "Most of the buildings are original, and the state government has had its seat here since 1777. So we're walking along the same paths, visiting the same buildings, and conducting the business of the state just as the contemporaries of George Washington might have done."

In Dover, history is a hands-on subject and the historic area, Old Dover, is a stage where the past comes to life in the here and now. Nate Davidson, an educator who works as a historic interpreter with the state Division of Parks and Recreation, literally plays the part of the characters he talks about. On a weekend evening, Davidson strolls The Green, dressed as a gentleman might in the late 1700s. When a small group gathers around, Davidson goes into character, pondering the significance of qualities such as liberty and freedom.

Until 2004, the numerous government offices, museums, galleries, and other businesses operated independently, and visitors to Old Dover had little idea what a great wealth the historic district had to offer. It was under the leadership of Gov. Ruth Ann Minner that a task force was established to lay the groundwork for the First State Heritage Park and make many of the historic buildings and sites it encompasses more visitor-friendly and accessible.

Today, what we have is a non-traditional "park without boundaries," a frame of mind more than geographical address. The idea was to increase the visibility of downtown Dover's attractions and foster among residents an appreciation for Delaware's heritage and a desire to protect it. While the park has no gates, fences, or walls, it has become a destination, drawing families from the Dover area and beyond with a look at Delaware history that is both colorful and fun.

Instead of listening to lectures, visitors converse with actors who portray characters from a wide variety of backgrounds and time periods. Portable audio wands are available with narrative keyed to historic sites and buildings, but even these are spoken by period actors and the recordings include background sounds that make the experience even more real.

The Heritage Park includes several anchor sites, most of which were owned by the state when the park was created. These include Legislative Hall, where the Delaware House of Representatives and Senate meets; the Legislative Mall; Delaware Public Archives; and the State House Museum, housed in the 1792 capitol building. Other buildings include the Kent County Courthouse, the Biggs Museum of American Art, the Delaware Archaeology Museum, and the Museum of Small Town Life, representing what a Delaware Main Street might have looked like in 1897.

One of the most unusual museums is the Eldridge Reeves Johnson Victrola Museum, which honors the Dover native who founded the Victor Talking Machine Company in 1901 in Camden, New Jersey. The museum houses many examples of phonographs, from early Thomas Edison models to elaborate and ornate examples made in the late 1920s and early '30s. Also on file are thousands of old recordings and other memorabilia from the early recorded music industry.

The nice thing about Old Dover is that it is pedestrian-friendly. A visitor can park the car, pick up an audio wand, and spend the day touring by foot. All of the attractions are within a few blocks of each other.

Dover is one of the fastest-growing cities on Delmarva, with the NASCAR speedway, Dover Downs, and a growing convention industry, but the old downtown still has the feel of a small, close-knit community. It's the kind of place those of us who live on Delmarva like to call home. It's rich in history and tradition, yet small enough to be comfortable, without pressure and pretence, which is another reason it would make a perfect capital of our 51st state.

On a mid-afternoon in early spring, I stood on The Green gazing at Legislative Hall and the line-up of old taverns and shops, and I noticed a faint but certain scent being carried by the breeze. I recognized it at once: the aroma of chicken manure carried by a stiff northwest breeze from a farm not far from town. Don't tell me you'll ever have experiences such as this in Richmond or Annapolis.

2

Come Fly With Me

The Air Force AMC Museum

I was at the controls of an Air Force C-5 cargo plane, making my final approach to the runway at Dover Air Force Base. "Nose up. Nose up," said my instructor. The huge aircraft was dropping slowly, the runway becoming larger, and the plane wanted to drift to the left. "Sidewind," someone muttered.

"More right rudder," said my coach. "Use your foot. Use your foot."

The runway was wide, a gray strip of concrete, green grass on either side. Within seconds, we would be down and my job was to keep it on the gray, not the green. "Push forward, then apply the brakes," he said.

Suddenly, we were on the ground and the plane came to a stop, not exactly in the center of the runway, but on the runway nonetheless. I took a deep breath. For someone who knows nothing about flying, who has never been at the controls of any kind of airplane, this is the perfect initiation: Get behind the controls of one of the largest aircraft in the world, and get it from the air to the ground without risking life and limb.

The pilot seat I was in was authentic, but the C-5 I was flying was not created by aircraft engineers, but rather software engineers who had done a wonderful job of making this virtual trip very exciting, but supremely safe. Unless I were to trip getting out of the seat, there was little chance of injury.

The flight simulator was in a hangar at the Air Mobility Command (or AMC) Museum in Dover, one of the jewels on Delmarva that too few people know about or appreciate. The AMC Museum is adjacent to the Dover Air Force Base, with the entrance on Route 9, a short distance past its junction with Route 113. I had driven by it numerous times when passing through Dover, but never thought about stopping, figuring you had to be a member of the military to get in.

"A lot of people have that notion, especially since 9/11 and all the stepped-up security at military bases," said museum director Mike Leister. "But we're separate from the Air Force Base and you can't get into the base from the museum grounds, so visitors don't have to go through any security checks. They just park in the parking lot and walk in. There's not even an entrance fee."

Dover Air Force Base has played a prominent role in modern military history, and the AMC Museum captures not only Dover's story, but also the broader spectrum of the Air Mobility Command. Dover AFB was opened in 1941, as America joined World War II, and the museum opened in 1986, with a single aircraft, a C-47A, that was literally plucked from the trash heap. Today the museum has more than two dozen aircraft, all of which have been carefully restored. The collection also includes numerous exhibits and an extensive archive for those doing research.

The hangar the museum calls home is an important historic site as well. The Army Air Force used the facility as a rocket test center during World War II and the building is on the National Register of Historic Places. Most of the aircraft in the museum collection were saved from the scrap heap and restored, often by volunteers who donated their time and expertise. In many cases, restoration took several years and required careful research and documentation.

"The C-47A was considered 'beyond salvage' by other museums when we got it," said Leister. "Today it is immaculately restored, complete with the D-Day invasion stripes it wore when it served with the 61st Troop Carrier Squadron in World War II."

Restoring the aircraft, known as the Turf and Sport Special, was more than a matter of cleaning it up, replacing parts, and applying fresh paint. "Restoration required a great deal of documentation," said Leister. "We found old photos and researched its combat history, and we were actually able to contact some of the crew that flew on it during the war. In 1990, we had a reunion here at the museum that included the D-Day pilot, the aerial engineer, and three of the 82nd Airborne Division paratroopers who jumped from it into St. Mere-Eglise on June 6, 1944."

The AMC Museum is home to a number of significant vintage aircraft, termed by Leister as the "first, last, and onlys." For example, there is the first C-141A, which first flew on December 17, 1963, sixty years to the day from the date of the Wright brothers' first flight. There is the last C-133B Cargomaster ever built, as well as the only surviving C-54M Skymaster, which was modified to haul coal during the Berlin Airlift. That aircraft has been restored to its original World War II condition, and Leister said there still is coal dust in the belly of the plane.

The AMC Museum collection fills not only the 20,000-square-foot hangar, but also the tarmac outside. Unlike most museums, there are few "do not touch" signs. Many of the aircraft are open to visitors, who are welcome to climb in, look around, and get a feeling for what it might have been like to have flown on one of these aircraft when they were in active duty.

As an Air Force veteran, I especially enjoyed visiting the C-130 Hercules. I flew as a passenger on one when returning from a temporary duty assignment in Brazil and immediately recalled how noisy and uncomfortable the aircraft was. We left Brasilia, the capital, early one morning headed for Florida, planning an overnight stopover in Trinidad along the way. Those of us onboard were looking forward to taking in the nightlife in Trinidad and perhaps sampling a few adult beverages, but after eight hours of high-decibel flight, and after sitting on those mesh-strap seats in the cargo hold all day, we checked into the hotel, lay down for a brief rest, and awoke just in time to catch the last leg of our flight the next morning.

3

Off to Bombay Hook

Route 9 Shows the Greener Side of Delaware

Route 9 is my avenue of choice when traveling north-south in Delaware. If you're traveling between Wilmington and Dover, Route 9 can be considered the green alternative to Route 13. The latter is probably the quickest way to travel between these cities, but it is not the most pleasant. Although traffic flows smoothly on the Route 1 bypass around Dover, Route 13 is often congested, with numerous traffic signals, commercial clutter, and traffic varying from high-speed commuters to slow-moving farm equipment.

Route 9 intersects with Route 113 south of Dover and generally parallels Route 13 all the way to New Castle and Wilmington. It is a handsome, two-lane roadway, lightly-traveled, and it introduces visitors to a decidedly quieter, more rural side of Delaware. Just outside Dover are the small fishing villages of Little Creek and Leipsic (pronounced LIP-sik), and there are working farms that grow soybeans and corn. Much of the land on the east side of Route 9 is protected as national wildlife refuge or state wildlife areas, and in many places Route 9 provides an open vista across thousands of acres of salt marsh separating the Delaware's mainland and Delaware Bay.

The best known of these refuges is Bombay Hook, which has been a national wildlife refuge since 1937 and is one of many of that particular vintage that provide a chain of rest stops for migrating waterfowl and shorebirds along the Atlantic Flyway. The shallow freshwater pools and salt marshes attract tens of thousands of geese and ducks, many of which spend the winter here before heading north in the spring.

At nearly 16,000 acres, Bombay Hook is a large preserve, and today the constituency goes far beyond waterfowl. In the summer, the ponds and flats attract black-necked stilts, glossy ibises, herons, egrets, sandpipers, and other shorebirds and wading birds. The wooded sections provide an important migratory corridor for warblers, tanagers, and other neotropical migrant songbirds. The agricultural fields and grassy meadows attract sparrows, bluebirds, and indigo buntings, among many others.

There is also the waterfowl. In the fall and winter, snow geese gather in the marshes and fields in flocks of thousands. There are Canada geese, black ducks, mallards, and

other dabbling ducks in the shallow pools, and the deeper tidal waters hold buffleheads, mergansers, loons, and other diving ducks.

Tina Watson is an outdoor recreation planner at the refuge, and on a balmy day in early spring we explored the impoundments to see how many waterfowl were sticking around and whether the spring migration of shorebirds had begun. The first of the impoundments, Raymond Pool, had black ducks, pintails, shovelers, widgeon, tundra swans, Canada geese, and green-winged teal. On the far side of the pond were avocets.

We drove along the earthen bank that created the impoundment and to the east we saw thousands of acres of salt marsh, interrupted only by George's Island in the distance. Mergansers, buffleheads, and other diving ducks were in the swift-moving tidal creeks, so we pulled over to check them out. "These dike roads were put in to create the impoundments, with water control structures added to control the depth of the water," Watson said. "So on one side we have shallow, freshwater ponds that attract dabbling ducks, and on the other side is a salt marsh, with deep creeks that have diving ducks. In fall, winter, and early spring, you can usually see large flocks of snow geese farther out in the marsh, and when the tide is low the mud flats can have hundreds of shorebirds."

As we looked on, great clouds of snow geese rose and fell on the far horizon. These birds would be leaving soon for breeding grounds in the far north. The tidal flats seemed barren until I scanned them with binoculars and found that they were alive with hundreds of small shorebirds — dunlin, we guessed — that were foraging on the exposed mud.

"The biologists manipulate the impoundments according to the season," Watson said. "They're probably lowering the water level now, and will let it drop more later in the spring. The waterfowl that have been here through the winter will be heading north to breed, and the shorebirds will be moving in. They like a wet surface where they can forage, but they can't hunt in deep water, so we maintain the water levels to suit the birds that are using the refuge at any particular time."

While the refuge was created to provide a sanctuary for migrating birds, there has long been a human involvement in the marshes and fields of Bombay Hook. Native Americans and early settlers fished for crabs in the tidal creeks, gathered oysters and clams, and hunted waterfowl in winter. The first recorded history of the Bombay Hook area began in 1697, when Mechacksett, Chief of the Kahansink, sold a tract of marshland to Peter Bayard of New York. Since then, salt hay has been harvested, fields planted, and ditches were dug to connect waterways and to ship goods to market.

The ponds at Bombay Hook were begun shortly after the refuge was created. A Civilian Conservation Corps (CCC) team stationed at nearby Leipsic began work on the dikes in the spring of 1938, and the crew stayed for nearly four years, until March 1942. The corps team was called Company 3269-C; it was the only African-American team to work in Delaware.

Company 3269-C was one of dozens of CCC teams that worked on wildlife refuges across America. The CCC was created in 1933 by President Franklin Roosevelt to provide jobs in the aftermath of the Great Depression. Until it was disbanded in 1942, the CCC provided employment for more than three million young men, including 250,000 African-Americans. Known as "Roosevelt's tree army," the corps planted an estimated three billion trees in the nine years it existed. The CCC worked on fifty-three wildlife refuges, building roads, dikes, and erecting buildings.

The dikes begun by the CCC workers in 1938 have been enlarged and improved upon over the years, and now the refuge has more than 1,000 acres of freshwater pools and timbered swamps. The refuge also has nearly 1,100 acres under cultivation, working with local farmers to produce crops that provide supplementary food for waterfowl and other migrating birds and mammals. A major portion of the refuge is occupied by forest and by vast expanses of pristine salt marsh, one of the most valuable natural areas in the Delaware Bay area.

Bombay Hook NWR covers a sizeable portion of the bayshore in Delaware. Refuge property begins along the Mahon River on the south and includes Kelly, Kent, and Bombay Hook islands, along with the marshes of Simons and Leipsic rivers and Duck Creek. The sluice ditch east of Bear Swamp Pool is the northern boundary. The refuge covers about eight miles of shoreline on the bay.

If you're unfamiliar with the refuge, the visitor center should be your first stop. There you can pick up a refuge map, guides to the trails, and an auto tour brochure. Most people see the refuge by car, which is something of a shame, because there are several good hiking paths and wooded areas that are full of warblers in the spring and fall. The car does come in handy in the summer, though, because the twelve miles of road are hot and dusty, and there's a good chance the insects will be out in force.

The refuge lends itself well to bicycle tours in the spring and fall, when the weather is cooperative and the bugs are dormant. The bike is a good compromise between the car, which lets you miss a lot of good stuff, and hiking, which can get tiring if you plan to cover all twelve miles of roads, plus the side trails.

The most accessible portions of the refuge are near the pools. The dike roadways provide access to the best birding and botanizing sections of Bombay Hook. From the visitor center, the road forks off to the right and makes a circle around Raymond Pool. A Boardwalk Trail, for hikers only, branches off the road, circles a small pond, and offers a great lookout over the salt marshes and a tidal stream that empties into the Leipsic River. This short trail is a good place to look for songbirds, especially when the warblers are moving through in the spring and fall.

The road continues north along Shearness Pool, which will be on the left, and the tidal salt marsh. A right turn will take you around Bear Swamp Pool, which usually has numerous shorebirds and a great concentration of black-crowned night herons during the warmer months. Bear Swamp Trail is a productive, short hike for migratory songbirds or resident birds.

Once around Bear Swamp Pool, you can drive down to Finis Pool, which in most seasons is a good idea. The wetlands, woods, and open meadows offer many different species of birds, depending upon the time of year. The pool here is fed by a freshwater stream, and the four hundred acres of woods nearby have been left largely undisturbed. So what we have here is a freshwater habitat suitable to a wide range of plants and animals. The woods has some of the largest trees on the refuge — sweet gum, white oak, and black tupelo — and the plants include jack-in-the-pulpit and pink lady slipper, which bloom in May. The forest is perhaps the best location on the refuge to watch migrating songbirds in the spring and summer. Bring along the binoculars, the field guide, and most important, don't forget the bug repellent.

4

Prime Hook

Delaware's Plum of a Wildlife Refuge

When the Dutch arrived at what is now Prime Hook National Wildlife Refuge in the 1600s, they discovered an abundance of purple beach plums and so they named the area Priume Hoek, meaning Plum Point. Over time, the Dutch pronunciation prevailed, and Prime Hook it is today.

Prime Hook NWR was created in 1963 to protect coastal wetlands for migrating waterfowl, but the constituency now goes beyond that. The refuge is managed for a diverse range of native wildlife, including birds, mammals, fish, reptiles, amphibians, insects, and plants. If you look at a map of Delaware, you'll see wide swaths of green along Delaware Bay and Delaware River. These would represent tens of thousands of acres of wetlands, ponds, and forests set aside for wildlife, either as national wildlife refuges or state wildlife management areas.

Of the two wildlife refuges along Delaware Bay — Prime Hook and Bombay Hook — the latter is better-known. Bombay Hook has numerous freshwater impoundments, miles of roads running along dikes, stunning views of saltwater wetlands, and easy access to a wide diversity of birding habitat. You can set up your scope, have a picnic lunch on the tailgate of your truck, and spend the afternoon viewing a great many birds without having to put on your hiking boots.

Prime Hook, several miles south of Bombay, also has birds, but it is a more interactive wildlife refuge, where visitors are encouraged to hit the trail, both by land and by water. There are a half-dozen hiking trails, plus a canoe trail that begins at the refuge visitor center and runs for some seven miles along Prime Hook Creek to Waples Mill Pond on Route 1.

My favorite trails are two that begin near the visitor center parking area. Dike Trail is a half-mile walkway paralleling the canal that links the parking area to Prime Hook Creek. The first part of the trail is wooded on both sides, a good place to look for songbirds. At about the half-way point, the forest gives way to open marsh and the vista changes completely. Suddenly, the view goes from dense woodland a few feet away to a sweeping brackish marsh that extends for miles in the distance.

A nice touch is the raised viewing platform at the end of the trail, providing a great look at the marsh meadow, Prime Hook Creek, and the beach communities in the distance. It was mid-October when I was there, and the waterfowl had already begun arriving. From the platform I could see a raft of several hundred dabbling ducks on the creek in the distance, and I made it a point to remember to bring a scope on my next visit.

Boardwalk Trail is equally interesting, but for different reasons. It's a half-mile loop that covers woodland, forested wetlands, open marsh, and old farm fields, all in a relatively short walk. If you want to see songbirds, this is the place to go. The trail begins on the edge of a swamp, and this edge habitat has numerous seed-producing plants: wild grape, greenbriar, holly, wax myrtle, sumac, poison ivy, and many others. Not surprisingly, many birds were flitting about in the understory.

From there the trail crosses an old farm field and then enters a bottomland swamp via a boardwalk. The swamp was dry when I was there in October, but there had been little rain for weeks, so in most seasons the boardwalk would be crossing a proper forested wetland. Wood ducks nest there in the spring.

The boardwalk emerges from woodland to open marsh, a landscape of reeds, grasses, and cattails, whose brown seed heads were numerous on this fall afternoon. This is perhaps the signature feature of Prime Hook...this landscape of brackish and freshwater marshland. The refuge has more than 8,000 acres of wetlands, and its 4,200-acre freshwater marsh is one of the largest on the East Coast, a great sanctuary for tens of thousands of migratory waterfowl each fall, and for shorebirds in spring and summer.

Before Prime Hook was a wildlife refuge, it was home to many farming families who settled in the area, and Boardwalk Trail provides evidence of this past life. As the trail nears its end, black walnut trees become numerous, the green seed casings covering the ground. These were part of the local family's orchard, no doubt joined by fruit trees and perhaps a grape arbor.

The Morris family lived not far from where the current visitor center is located, and although the old homestead was long-ago claimed by age and neglect, several generations of Morrises remain. The family cemetery is just off Boardwalk Trail, the eight remaining tombstones protected by a metal fence. The stones are weathered and chalky, with dates of the deceased ranging from 1818 to 1864.

The old cemetery provides evidence of the passage of time, of the generational changes this land has seen. Today it is a wildlife refuge, but not long ago it supported families who farmed the land, hunted the marsh, and fished the waters. Before that, it was settled by Dutch explorers who reveled in the discovery of plums growing wild on the beach and, before that, the land and waters we know today as Prime Hook sustained many generations of Great Sicconese Lenape Indians who lived and hunted here. It would be interesting to know what name they gave this land.

5

Historic Lewes

The First State's First Town

If you turn on Front Street in Lewes, drive past the shops and historic homes, you'll follow the Delaware Bay shoreline northward and discover a stone monument on your right commemorating the first Dutch settlement by Devries in 1631. "Here was the cradling of a state," the monument reads, somewhat modestly.

By the time you get to the monument, Front Street will have become Pilot Town Road, and the setting will have changed from shops and restaurants to boatyards and marinas, to salt marsh and tidal creeks flowing into distant woodland. Delaware Bay is a short distance away, and if you use the binoculars, you can see a half-dozen or more freighters out there, some with cargo containers, some with bellies full of crude oil. The ships in the distance are hazy and odd looking, with only the topsides visible beyond the curvature of the earth.

This is a good place to begin a tour of Lewes because it epitomizes what the focal point of this community always has been. Lewes is a seafaring town, and not necessarily one of polished mahogany, white sneakers, and blue blazers. Lewes is a town of Dutch whalers, pilots and traders, and pirates and cargo masters. Work on the water here has been gritty and knuckle-scraping hard, where wind in the sails meant profit, and not necessarily pleasure.

This places Lewes in context. I drove back downtown, had a grilled scallop sandwich with roasted red pepper aioli at Jerry's Seafood, and thought about Captain Kidd visiting in the late 1600s, the British Navy attacking the town in 1813, and before that, conflicts with the Lenni Lenape Indians that left many of the original settlers massacred.

Back on the sidewalk, Second Street was bustling with activity. A man and woman, both with long ponytails, walked a pair of huge German shepherds. One shop advertised specials on handmade woolen sweaters, another specials on handmade soaps, and I stopped in at a third, selling international foods, to buy dessert, a box of British candies called Smarties, which are at once fruity and chocolatey.

It's easy to visit Lewes and get lost amid shops, seafood restaurants, antique stores, art galleries, and all sorts of side streets to explore, wonderful architecture to behold,

friendly people who greet you on the sidewalk even though they've never seen you before in their lives. However, I was looking for evidence of the old hard side of Lewes, the rough-knuckle, Pilot Town Road-side of Lewes.

A shopkeeper directed me to a small park on Front Street, where cannons were aimed seaward to defend against the British. One such cannon was confiscated from a pirate ship, she told me. Farther along Front Street was Cannonball House, so named because a cannonball the size of a softball was wedged into the brickwork of the foundation, compliments of the British Navy in 1813. Next door was the site of the original maritime exchange, where men with telescopes stood on look-out towers, identifying ships that approached the harbor.

A block away, back on Second Street, I found the Ryves Holt House, built around 1665. It's the oldest house in Delaware and could tell some hard-knuckle stories. Next to that is St. Peter's Episcopal Church, a comparatively new building constructed around 1858. It is, however, the third church on the site, as witnessed by a stroll through the church cemetery, which has the tombs of Margaret Huling, born in 1631, and Elizabeth H. Cullen, "born February 30, 1760."

The cemetery also is the resting place of Captain James Drew, who holds a prominent place in the seafaring tradition of Lewes. Drew was skipper of the *De*

M.A. CLARKE

Braak, a sloop-of-war of the Royal Navy that escorted a convoy to America in February 1798. On May 28th, the *De Braak* and a Spanish ship she had captured rounded Cape Henlopen and headed for Lewes when a freak storm blew in. The *De Braak* went down, and with her Captain Drew, thirty-four crew members, and twelve Spanish prisoners.

Around the corner from St. Peter's, on Mulberry Street, is the original Methodist meetinghouse, locally known as the "traveling meetinghouse." It was built on the corner of Third and Market streets around 1790, and in 1828 was moved to Mulberry and Church streets. In 1870, it traveled to its present location and has not budged since.

Out on King's Highway, the main route leading from Route 1 to downtown Lewes, is the Zwaanendael Museum, one of the most distinctive buildings in town. The museum was built in 1931 by the state of Delaware to honor the ill-fated Dutch settlement of 1631. The building is based upon the design of the city hall, or Stadhuis, of Hoorn, Holland. Among the exhibits are artifacts from the *De Braak*. The museum, it seems to me, is a good place to end a visit to Lewes. After all the wonderful architecture, the history, the shops, and the restaurants, it is fitting to remember Lewes by this monument to the few brave Dutchmen who landed on these shores in 1631, creating what became the first town in the first state.

6

Cape Henlopen

A Sandy Search for a Snowy Owl

A few years ago I nearly stepped on a snowy owl on the beach at Cape Henlopen State Park. I was walking with my head down, looking for something interesting in the sand, when the owl and I surprised each other. I thought at first it was an old white garbage bag sitting there, and then it lifted a wing. I don't know what the owl thought.

Unfortunately, that was the last time I saw a snowy owl, much less stepped on one, and so on a long winter weekend we decided to go back and see if there were still any owls on that beach. My wife, Lynn, and son, Tom, had never seen one, and Lynn was keen to add one to her life list. Tom was sixteen at the time and sat in the backseat and read *Guitar World*.

Cape Henlopen is shaped like an upside-down comma. The little tail of the comma sticks out into Delaware Bay, separating it from the Atlantic Ocean, so you can walk down one side of the comma on the bay and return on the other side along the ocean. The little tip of the comma is a good place to find snowy owls.

One thing we hadn't anticipated when we left home, though, was that the wind was going to be blowing out of the north around forty knots, right in our faces as we hiked toward the point. This not only made things uncomfortable, but it also made visibility very poor. Fine sand hung in the air like a morning mist, a thick, abrasive cloud. If I had been watching this scene on TV, no doubt it would have been lovely, sand skittering across the spit, piling up in wind shadows behind the dunes, sunlight breaking through clouds in golden shafts.

I leaned into the wind and wished I'd brought my duck hunting clothes instead of the Barbour˚ jacket, which is very nice as long as it's not windy. Lynn and I pressed on, looking for old white garbage bags that sometimes lifted a wing. We scoured the beach with the binoculars and peered into the dunes as best we could. (They're closed to hikers to prevent damage to vegetation.) Tom actually seemed to be having a good time. He brought along a new camera and was photographing the sunlight breaking through the clouds, casting shadows on the dunes.

We made it to the tip, hiked along the ocean side, and realized that on this particular day we were unlikely to see a snowy owl. On the way back, we had the wind behind us.

Cape Henlopen State Park has more to offer than snowy owls, so we decided to explore. The park is among the oldest public lands in America. In 1682, William Penn declared that the lands of the Cape were for the common use of the citizens of Lewes and Sussex Counties, thus establishing the nation's first public parks. Cape Henlopen served as a military base during World War II, and for centuries the old lighthouse and breakwater provided guidance and safe harbor for sailors.

The military presence is easily recognized today. Most of the park roads are of World War II vintage concrete. Bunkers and former gun emplacements are tucked into dunes and bluffs, and concrete look-out towers provide a sweeping view of the entrance to Delaware Bay. A former barracks has been renovated and is now used as an environmental education center.

In the summer, the big draw here is the ocean beach, and the campground is usually filled with vacationing families. In winter and early spring, the park gets weekend hikers and bicyclists. The park has several miles of paved bike paths, one of which leads to the top of a bluff overlooking the ocean, presenting a view well worth the uphill grind.

Birders will flock to the park in April and May to witness the annual horseshoe crab and shorebird phenomenon. The crabs lumber ashore on the bayside of the spit to lay eggs, and the birds will soon follow, feasting on the eggs as they travel to breeding grounds in the Arctic.

The Nature Center, near the park entrance, is a good place to begin a trip to Cape Henlopen. Books, maps, and brochures are available, and interpretive displays provide a look at the bay/ocean ecosystem of the cape. Information is also available on programs and nature tours led by staff naturalists.

Our most recent visit to Cape Henlopen did not produce a snowy owl, but if the bird were commonplace and easy to find, it wouldn't be special. The snowy owl carries a certain aura of mystery and intrigue. It is a large white owl that spends most of its life on the open tundra of the Arctic, preying chiefly on lemmings. In the dead of winter, when the lemming population ebbs, the birds sometimes retreat from their northern range, a move necessitated by hunger. That's when we have a chance to see them.

"Look at it this way," said Lynn. "It's disappointing not to see a snowy owl, but from the birds' point of view, the fact that they're not here is probably good news."

Lewes to Rehoboth

All Aboard the Junction and Breakwater

I have little affection for traffic congestion and commercial sprawl, so driving Route 1 in the Lewes/Rehoboth area is not my idea of a day at the beach. I prefer hiking trails to outlet malls any day. Make my lunch a mushy PBJ in the boonies, not red meat and flaccid fries in a shopping strip sports bar.

Apparently, I'm not the only pilgrim out there who feels that way. How else to explain the Junction and Breakwater Trail, a path that links Lewes and Rehoboth, an avenue on which you can actually ride a bicycle from the Rehoboth resort area to Lewes without leaving a tire mark on Route 1? Incredible! You could even ride a bike from Rehoboth to Lewes, get on the Cape May ferry, and spend the night in New Jersey without dodging fendered machines.

The first time I tried the Junction and Breakwater, I was a bit doubtful. Here we have one of the fastest-growing areas in southern Delaware, soybean fields being converted to parking lots at warp speed, and someone actually is going to put a bike path through all this. The website promised a ride of woody tranquility, so I decided to investigate, with sort of a "yeah, right" sneer in a dark corner of my mind.

I stopped in at Jim Bellas' Bike to Go shop in downtown Rehoboth, picked up a map and cue sheet, and set off. The first few bits were your basic suburban bike path, a paved lane attached to a roadway, with little bike figures painted in white to make it official. Soon, though, I crossed Holland Glade Road, found myself pedaling through a farm field, then into pine woods, and then along a cut-over cornfield complete with farmhouse, barn, and silo in the distance. Toto, I don't think we're on Route 1 anymore. Here I was in the "Wizard of Odd."

Route 1 was out there, somewhere, but in only a few minutes I had left behind traffic and outlet malls and was suddenly back in 1952, longing for my "I Like Ike" button. It was surreal.

Many years ago, a short-line railroad ran between Lewes and Rehoboth, and it was called the Junction and Breakwater. The trail I was riding follows a portion of the original rail bed, and this explains the rather curious name. It is one of three rail trails in Delaware, and the longest, with a distance of about ten miles, factoring in the suburban bike paths and various spurs.

The north and south portions of the Junction and Breakwater run along roadways in residential communities, but the central part of the trail is the most interesting. It was here that the railroad ran many years ago. Coming from Rehoboth, I biked through forests and farm fields, and then onto a trestle that crossed Holland Glade. The view was surprising, considering the density of development in the Rehoboth area. A small creek flowed under the bridge, branching off to the west and disappearing into woods. To the east, a salt marsh meadow stretched away to the horizon. Wildflowers were in bloom and a phoebe was perched atop a sumac tree, flicking its tail the way phoebes do.

From here I rode north to Wolfe Neck, the trail running through a forest of pine and mixed hardwoods. I met a few other bike riders and a jogger or two, but on a warm fall weekday I had the trail nearly to myself. Another trestle crosses a creek and salt marsh at Wolfe Neck, and from here the trail rejoins suburbia, heading through a subdivision toward Lewes and Cape Henlopen State Park.

The official trail head is just south of the trestle, on the west side of the trail. Take a little spur here and you'll find a parking lot, restrooms, bike rack, and information kiosk, all on the site of the 1887 Wolfe Farm, with a farmhouse and outbuildings that are being restored. The remains of an old barn, built with posts hewn from native cedar, is along the trail, and when I visited a huge persimmon tree stood just outside the parking lot, heavy with ripe orange fruit on a sunny October day.

The Junction and Breakwater seems to serve two constituencies. It is a great commuter path for local folks who want to travel between Lewes and Rehoboth without firing up the car, and it also is a welcome escape path for people who want to spend a few hours in a quiet, wooded setting surprisingly close to an intensely developed commercial area. The core of the trail, the stretch between Holland Glade and Wolfe Glade, is quiet, wooded, and wild. May it long remain so.

8

Trap Pond State Park

Riding Through a Shower of Leaves

One of the best places to go for a bike ride on Delmarva is Loblolly Trail, a five-mile pathway that winds through Trap Pond State Park, four miles east of Laurel, Delaware, and the best time to go is fall or early winter, when the bugs are dormant, the summer campers have gone home, and the leaves are paying one final tribute to the growing season.

I went in mid-October, stopping at the camp store to pay my out-of-state parking fee, and then got on the trail at the crosswalk just beyond the store entrance. There was a slight breeze and leaves were falling like huge, amber flakes of snow, accumulating on the path until it was nearly indistinguishable from the undergrowth.

Loblolly Trail loops around the park, and around Trap Pond, here and there offering nice views of what, by Delmarva standards, is a pretty good size lake. On the park map, the trail looks like a fairly standard loop, but once you get on the bike and start pedaling, you realize that it is a narrow, twisty pathway that requires your full attention, especially when the oaks and sweet gums begin to cover it with leaves.

It is, in a word, fun. There are a few straight stretches, but none to induce boredom, and nearly the entire trail winds through a pine and hardwood forest, making for a beautiful venue and rendering any wind that may be blowing inconsequential.

Trap Pond State Park, of course, offers more than a biking/hiking trail. There are campgrounds, small cabins, picnic areas, boat launch facilities, a canoe trail, and outstanding fishing, but I wanted to explore the park by bike, and Loblolly Trail showcases much that the park has to offer: the old cypress swamp, upland forest, the pond, and even a country church and cemetery.

I headed east at the camp store crosswalk and was immediately zigzagging through giant pines, hardwoods, and hollies. At three-quarters of a mile, I came to a "T," where a left turn would take me to a dead-end at Goose Neck Road, so I turned right, headed south, and entered a hardwood swamp. There had been little rain and the vernal pools and swampy areas were high and dry. Water was flowing through one shallow creek, and the system of bridges and walkways provided a great view. I made a mental note to come back in the spring when the swamp is inundated and the wildflowers are in bloom.

After another mile or so, I came to an intersection with Boundary Trail. A right turn would have taken me back to the campground area and reduced my ride by more than two miles, but I was still entranced by riding through falling leaves, and so kept straight, soon arriving at the backyard of a little country church on Whaley's Road. It was a handsome little place of worship, white frame, not currently in use, but undergoing repair. The cemetery had the graves of numerous local families, some of the headstones dating back to the mid-nineteenth century. There were familiar Delmarva names: Hudson, Pusey, Matthews, Thompson, Wootten, Lecates, Swain, and many others.

I got back on the trail and, after riding through woods for about two and a half miles, arrived at Wootten Road, just across from Raccoon Pond, an appendage of Trap Pond. A couple of quick right turns took me back into the woods, and here the trail ran alongside the pond, visible through the thinning leaves. The trail skirted the southern edge of the pond and, after about four miles, I was back among civilization. Along the shoreline were picnic tables, grilling stands, restrooms, and the Bald Cypress Nature Center, which was closed when I visited. In the far corner of the picnic area was a boathouse where canoes and kayaks could be rented during the summer season.

From there Loblolly Trail skirts the northwest boundary of the pond, crossing the dike and spillway that created the pond many years ago and providing a great overlook as Trap Pond stretched toward the horizon.

At five miles, I was back at the truck, my ride finished, complete with a few short detours. It was a comparatively short ride, but totally entertaining the entire way. The trail is mostly narrow and winding, and the surface is hard-packed clay and gravel — a nice surface for off-road bikes or hybrids, perhaps a bit squirrelly for road bikes. The trail is level, by no means a mountain biking trail, nor is it something advanced riders would use for an aerobic workout. It is, above all, an entertaining trail for riders of all skill levels. If it's a workout you're looking for, you could ride it twice.

9

The DuPont Nature Center

At Slaughter Beach, Horseshoe Crabs are a Hit

Some consider them rather homely looking, others think they are fearsome, and at least one writer has likened them to World War I army helmets crawling across the beach. However you see them, horseshoe crabs — those round, spikey-tailed critters of Delmarva's seaside — are an important part of the ecology of the bays and creeks that line our coast.

Many people have lived on Delmarva for years without even seeing a horseshoe crab, and a good number of people who have seen them have no idea of the role they play in the natural system of the estuary. The state of Delaware decided to do something about that lack of awareness in 2007, when it opened the DuPont Nature Center at Mispillion Harbor, at the site of the old Mispillion Lighthouse, which was struck by lightning and burned in 2002.

The DuPont Center is hard to miss. If you're driving from Milford to Slaughter Beach, turn left on Lighthouse Road just before entering the community of Slaughter Beach. Lighthouse Road comes to an uncelebrated end in the parking lot of a building set high on pilings, sporting a bright red roof, complete with red cupola. If you want to learn more about horseshoe crabs, climb the steps and walk in.

When I visited, Dawn Webb, the manager of the center, was preparing for a visit by local schoolteachers the next day. Webb had set up folding tables and chairs and was distributing information packets on the horseshoe crab and its role in the natural system of the Delaware estuary. "Science and education are our missions," said Webb. "We have groups of school children come through, we have teachers, and of course we have family groups stop by when they're visiting the area."

A deck surrounds the building, which formerly was Lighthouse Restaurant, and from it you can see sandy beaches where female horseshoe crabs will lumber ashore each spring and lay masses of green eggs, which will be fertilized by males that follow the females ashore. Of the millions of eggs laid on the beach, precious few survive to become adult horseshoe crabs. Most are eaten by birds, most notably the red knot, a small shorebird and tenacious traveler that depends upon horseshoe crab eggs to fuel its journey from its winter home in South America to breeding grounds in the Arctic.

An estimated 30,000 red knots descend upon Delaware beaches in May and early June, desperate for food to fuel their journey. "Red knots will weigh about 100 grams (3-1/2 ounces) when they arrive here, but when they leave a few weeks later they'll weigh more than 200 grams (7 ounces)," said Webb. "And they'll need every gram (ounce) of it to sustain them on the remaining flight and on the frozen nesting grounds where food will be scarce early in the breeding season."

The location of the DuPont Center is ideal for teaching visitors about horseshoe crabs and other natural features of the Delaware estuary. It stands amid one of the most productive horseshoe crab nesting sites on the Mid-Atlantic Coast, and a remote camera on a beach 100 yards away broadcasts real-time images of nesting crabs and foraging red knots to a plasma viewing screen in the center.

"We have state-of-the-art electronics," said Webb. "We can even do a virtual fly-over with the computer, giving the viewer an aerial look at the estuary and the shoreline. Most of the exhibits are interactive, so the kids really like them, and the adults as well."

The DuPont Center is not strictly about horseshoe crabs. Exhibits interpret the history of nearby Milford and Slaughter Beach, as well as the Mispillion Lighthouse, which was built in 1873. There are displays on bird identification and exhibits that demonstrate the tremendous diversity of the Delaware estuary, which begins in Trenton, New Jersey, and runs southward through the Delaware River and Delaware Bay, past Cape Henlopen, where it joins the Atlantic Ocean.

There are also programs to attend. When I visited, a kayak tour had just ended, but a presentation on the commercial history of the Delaware Bay was coming up. Hunting season was just beginning, and the center was preparing a program on Delaware's whitetail deer population. Fittingly, in a building that once housed a restaurant, the program on deer included wild game recipes and cooking demonstrations — and you didn't even have to leave a tip.

41

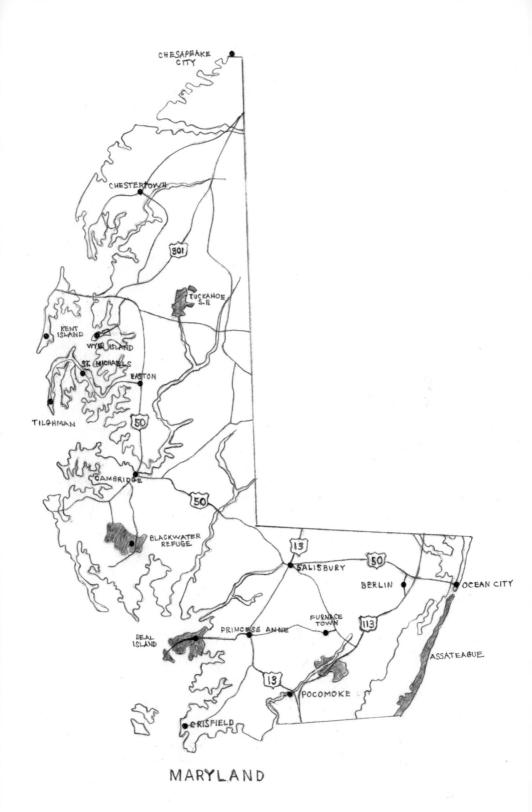

CHESAPEAKE
CITY

CHESTERTOWN

301

TUCKAHOE
S.R.

KENT
ISLAND

WYE ISLAND

ST. MICHAELS

EASTON

50

TILGHMAN

CAMBRIDGE

50

BLACKWATER
REFUGE

13

SALISBURY

50

BERLIN

OCEAN CITY

FURNACE
TOWN

113

DEAL
ISLAND

PRINCESS ANNE

ASSATEAGUE

13

POCOMOKE

CRISFIELD

MARYLAND

Maryland Adventures

■ ■ ■

About seventy-five percent of the Maryland trips described here have something to do with the water. We canoe on the Pocomoke River and Nassawango Creek, we go sailing, fishing, camping on the beach, crabbing, and we even witnessed a lunar eclipse from an oceanfront hotel room. This is not to mention speculating about local history on the waterfront in Chestertown, Oxford, Kent Island, and Wye Island.

Maryland has a great wealth of waterfront. On the Chesapeake Bay are wonderful places, such as Queen Anne's County, the gateway to the Eastern Shore, as well as numerous rivers that empty into the bay and towns, such as St. Michaels, Easton, Rock Hall, Chestertown, and Oxford, where the landscape has shaped the history and culture of the region.

Farther south are Blackwater National Wildlife Refuge, Crisfield, and Deal Island, uncrowded sanctuaries where men still work on the water and bald eagles soar over vast salt meadows.

On the eastern portion of the state are the beach resorts, Ocean City and its famous Boardwalk, the hotels and restaurants, the summertime getaways, and, in our case, a special one during the winter. There is Assateague, with its miles of wild beach, wildlife, wild ponies, and places where you can gather clams for chowder or catch a dozen or so crabs to steam for dinner.

In between Chesapeake Country and the Atlantic Coast are wonderful little towns, such as Snow Hill on the Pocomoke River; Berlin, with its great Christmas celebration; Princess Anne; and, of course, Salisbury, Maryland's center for shopping and entertainment and home to professional baseball, Salisbury University, the Ward Museum, and Delmarva's only zoo. Delmarva's newest museum, the Delmarva Discovery Center, opened on the riverfront in Pocomoke City in a 1920s-vintage building, and it is quickly becoming one of the gems of southern Maryland. The goal of the center is the preservation and interpretation of local culture and natural heritage, and it traces life on Delmarva from the time of the Native Americans to modern day.

Maryland is a wealthy state, rich in natural resources, rich in history, and blessed with a landscape that has shaped the history and culture of this land for generations. The Maryland portion of Delmarva is a place you can visit over and over again, and find something new each time you come.

10

Chesapeake City

Life, Death, and Rebirth of Delmarva's Canal Town

I was standing on the grassy bank of the Chesapeake and Delaware (C & D) Canal, on the grounds of the Canal Museum, and I was watching a sailboat pass through, heading west to east, from the Chesapeake Bay to the Delaware River. The wind was dead calm, the sail was down, and the boat was under motor power. Four people were in the cockpit of the boat, all of them spread across cushions in the shade of a blue Bimini top. Three appeared to be dozing while the fourth remained sufficiently upright to man the tiller and keep the boat headed in a straight line for the next fifteen miles. What a relaxing way to spend the day, I thought. As the boat passed by, I noticed the name painted on the stern: "Tranquility."

To many of us, the C & D Canal helps define the Delmarva Peninsula, providing its unofficial northern boundary. It begins on the west at Elk River, near the Chesapeake Bay, and runs for some thirty miles across Maryland and Delaware until it joins the Delaware River south of Wilmington. If you're looking for a line to define the beginning and ending of Delmarva, the canal provides a handy blue boundary on the state highway map — and the boundary is a cultural as well as a geographical feature. Cross the canal and head north to Newark, Wilmington, and Philadelphia, and you're definitely in an urban setting. Drive along I-95 and you quickly realize you are no longer on Delmarva. Those tranquil rivers and farmsteads and fields of grain have been replaced by interstate commerce.

The purpose of the canal, of course, was not to provide us with a handy boundary line to define Delmarva. The canal was dug to link Baltimore and other bay ports with Wilmington and Philadelphia on the Delaware River. Without the canal, ships would have to sail down the bay, through the Virginia capes, and then north up the coast — a long and sometimes dangerous journey. With the canal, the distance between the bay and the Delaware River is about thirty miles.

The idea for the canal came along years before the Revolutionary War, but work on the project didn't actually begin until 1824. It was completed five years later. As work on the canal progressed, a village grew around the lock and the great steam-powered pump that controlled the water level. Stores opened to sell merchandise to workers and canal officials. Lodging was needed. Taverns opened for business. People moved in and built homes and churches. Before long, a village stood on the banks of the canal.

In the 1830s, shortly after the canal opened, the community was called Bohemia Village. As commerce on the canal flourished, more people moved in, business grew, and Bohemia became a thriving shipping center. Sometime around 1850, for reasons unknown, the name Bohemia Village was dropped in favor of Chesapeake City, a somewhat ambitious title for a village with only a few hundred permanent residents.

Chesapeake City became a busy port town, and numerous local residents made a great deal of money in coal, lumber, agricultural products, and shipping. Fine homes were built, and the town became a regular stop for the famous showboat "The Adams Floating Theatre."

The federal government purchased the canal in 1929, a century after it opened, and the C & D was widened from its original sixty-six feet, the locks were removed, and the canal was dredged to accommodate ships with greater drafts. These "improvements" took several of the town streets, and they took a toll on the commerce Chesapeake City had enjoyed for a hundred years. With the locks removed, ships sailed through town without stopping and potential trade passed the town by. Gradually, businesses closed, people moved away, and Chesapeake City fell on hard times. A further blow came in 1948 when the high-rise bridge opened, carrying traffic up and over the little town, giving potential visitors a less than compelling view of various rooftops. Chesapeake City, it seemed, would slowly decay and become another ghost town, a reminder of an earlier era of shipping and commerce on Delmarva.

However, some Chesapeake City residents realized their town still had potential, not as a working canal town, but as a part of maritime history. If the town were restored, visitors would come, businesses would open, and Chesapeake City would thrive once again, but with a different clientele.

If you're driving north on Maryland Route 213 in Cecil County, do yourself a favor and take the exit just before the high-rise bridge. Take a right on First Street, continue around to Pell Gardens, park along the waterfront, and spend an enjoyable day exploring one of the real undiscovered jewels of Delmarva. Chesapeake City is spiffed up and ready for company. Most of the nineteenth-century homes have been restored, with welcoming porches and colors that challenge the visual spectrum. There are restaurants, antique shops, and galleries. A busy marina is adjacent to the park, and just across the anchorage basin is the U.S. Corps of Engineers Canal Museum housed in the original pumping station that was used when the canal had locks and a towpath. Here, you can learn how Chesapeake City was born and how it grew. Afterwards, go out and explore the tree-lined streets and shops and you will discover that when business and commerce change, now and then it happens with a happy ending.

11

Chestertown

High Street, High Tea, and a Dunk in the Chester River

If someone gave out awards for Delmarva towns that best reflect their British heritage, Chestertown would be a no-brainer. Chestertown has been Kent County's seat of government since 1706, and, given its location on the Chester River, it served as the royal port of entry during the days when Maryland was a colony. Chestertown was the scene of its own Revolutionary War tea party in 1774, and the main thoroughfare leading from the river to the business district is called the High Street, in good British fashion. Along High Street is a proper town square, complete with huge shade trees, a fountain, and ample benches where one can sit and watch the commerce of Chestertown unfold.

A walking tour of Chestertown is a great way to spend a day, and if you come in October, you can even enjoy the Tea Time House Tour featuring heritage homes open to the public. They very likely serve scones and clotted cream along with the cup of Earl Grey.

Like most small towns on Delmarva, Chestertown has spread away from its early hub, which would be the few blocks made up by High, Cross, Maple, Water, Queen, and Spring streets, where business has been conducted for more than three hundred years. Drive up Route 213 and you'll see fast-food chains, shopping centers, hotels, and many other facilities in various stages of construction. For those of us who are interested in history and architecture, though, the old downtown is the place to explore, and the best way to do so is by foot.

Chestertown grew up along its port, where tobacco and later grains were brought from nearby farms to be shipped to market. Chestertown was one of six official ports of entry, so designated in 1706 by the Maryland General Assembly under pressure from the British Crown. Taxes were collected on goods being shipped to and from the port, and they were assessed in the custom house, which at that time was along the river at High Street. The original custom house is no longer standing, but its replacement, built at the corner of High and Water streets in 1746, can be seen today.

In May of 1774, not far from the custom house, a group of local residents became enraged over the closing of the Port of Boston because of its "tea party," and boarded the custom collector's brigantine and dumped its cargo of tea into the Chester River. This small act of civil disobedience was followed a year later by outright revolution, when America began its war for independence from Great Britain.

Old Chestertown is a community of wide streets and red-brick sidewalks, some slightly rumpled by the roots of giant sycamores that have shaded many generations of Chestertown's business leaders and their constituents. A good place to begin a tour here is along the waterfront, where you can see homes built in the eighteenth century by some of the merchants and shipbuilders that helped give life to Chestertown. At 1010 North Water Street is Widehall, built around 1770 by Thomas Smythe, reputed at that time to be Kent County's wealthiest resident.

Across High Street, farther along Water Street, are numerous other homes from the same general period, providing visitors with an education in eighteenth-century architecture within a walk of a few hundred feet.

Although Chestertown has spread away from the river, the business of Kent County is still conducted in the old part of town. The courthouse is on Cross Street, across from the town hall, and Emmanuel Episcopal Church is just down the street. It was here that a group of Anglican clergymen convened with the rector of Chester Parish in 1780 to adopt a new title that would signify the break from England — here the Protestant Episcopal Church of the United States was formed.

Chestertown is home to the first college chartered in the nation after the signing of the Declaration of Independence. The college was founded by Rev. William Smith, the Chester Parish rector, in 1782. Named for one of the heroes of the Revolution and our first commander-in-chief, Washington College has played a leading role in the educational and cultural life of Chestertown for many years; the campus is just north of the old part of town.

Before heading up to the campus, you might want to visit one more home, which should definitely be on Chestertown's Tea Time House Tour in October. This would be the Geddes-Piper House, a three-story town home dating from 1780. Here lived William Geddes, Chestertown's very own collector of customs, whose shipload of Earl Grey was added to the flotsam of the Chester River on May 23, 1774.

12

Eastern Neck
National Wildlife Refuge

Not Just for the Birds

Eastern Neck National Wildlife Refuge, near Rock Hall, is well known among birdwatchers for the flocks of waterfowl that gather there each winter. However, what many people don't realize is that Eastern Neck is one of the best places on Delmarva to see another type of flying critter, and the best time to do so is during the dog days of summer.

Go to Eastern Neck in July and August and you'll see thousands of butterflies of many different species. The refuge has planted a large butterfly garden, and the trail that loops through it provides an excellent venue for spotting dozens of different species, from tiny skippers to colorful tiger swallowtails and monarchs. In fact, butterfly-watching is good throughout the refuge. In late summer, the flowering plants of the brackish marsh are in bloom, and these are natural butterfly attractants. The boardwalk that leads to the Tubby Cove observation platform is a perfect place to see butterflies, as it puts you just a few feet above a variety of flowering plants and the insects they attract.

Eastern Neck is a 2,285-acre island, connected to the mainland by a small wooden bridge about six miles from the town of Rock Hall. Take state Route 445 and head south; when the road ends, you'll be in the wildlife refuge.

Eastern Neck is a popular destination from October through February, when tens of thousands of waterfowl gather in the shallow bays and ponds of the refuge. At the peak of the season, some 40,000 waterfowl will be on the refuge, with thirty-two different species on record. Canada geese head the list, with an estimated winter population of 20,000, but the refuge also has a large population of canvasback ducks, an increasingly rare sight on Delmarva, and tundra swans gather by the thousands.

Eastern Neck also attracts many songbirds during the spring and fall migration. The woodlands and shrub thickets will have numerous species of warblers, thrushes, tanagers, flycatchers, and many others. The bird list published by the refuge names nearly 250 bird species seen at some time during the year, so if you want to see birds, go to Eastern Neck from October through February. If you want to see butterflies, go during the peak of summer. Take along the repellent, because there likely will be flying insects that are attracted to humans as well as flowering plants.

While many of our coastal wildlife refuges date from the 1930s and '40s, Eastern Neck is a bit newer than that. It was created between 1962 and 1967, shortly after a developer bought a large tract and created a subdivision of 293 small lots. Opposition to the development led to the eventual purchase of the entire island by the U.S. Fish and Wildlife Service to protect its valuable wildlife habitat. Today, the only residence ever built in the "Cape Chester" subdivision serves as housing for researchers and temporary workers.

Eastern Neck is popular among those of us who enjoy watching wildlife, and the boat landing at Bogles Wharf provides water access for recreational fishing and for exploring the nearby Eastern Neck Island water trail. Long before the refuge was created, however, Eastern Neck played a colorful role in the history of Kent County.

Native Americans lived mostly on the mainland, but foraged on Eastern Neck, leaving behind shell middens, pottery, and stone tools. Capt. John Smith explored the area in 1608, meeting members of the Ozinie tribe, relatives of the Nanticokes, who were well-known for beadwork made of local oyster and clam shells. Sadly, members of the Ozinie did not last long after this original contact. In less than one hundred years they were wiped out because of introduced diseases and warfare.

European presence on the island began between 1658 and 1680 when Col. Joseph Wickes and his partner, Thomas Hynson, were granted various tracts until they owned the entire island. Wickes built a mansion on the south end of the island, which was regarded as one of the finest homes in the area. Wickes, who eventually bought out Hynson, grew tobacco and other crops, which were shipped to market on vessels built in his family's shipyard. His grandson, Lambert Wickes, was a naval hero during the Revolutionary War and was lost at sea when his ship went down in a storm off the Newfoundland coast while returning from France. A monument to Wickes is located near the old home site on the south end of the refuge.

The island remained under the ownership of various members of the Wickes family until 1902. A small fishing village was located at Bogles Wharf, with an oyster packinghouse and a steamboat wharf nearby. By the 1920s, wealthy waterfowl hunters from nearby cities had discovered the island and they purchased tracts and built hunting lodges. One lodge, built in 1930 with cedar siding and a slate roof, still stands and today serves as a visitor center and office for refuge staff.

With the creation of the wildlife refuge in the 1960s, the island seems to have achieved a level of stability. There will never be a large residential development, and waterfowl these days are hunted with a camera and telephoto lens. Still, there is a steady stream of visitors, people who appreciate flocks of hundreds of canvasbacks in the winter, and perhaps a solitary zebra swallowtail fluttering by in the summer.

13

Rock Hall

Sailing Away on the Upper Chesapeake

The amazing thing about sailing on a substantial boat is how a vehicle of such weight and mass can move so quietly and effortlessly on just the hint of a summer breeze. A party of six had joined Capt. Mark and Suzanne Einstein on their thirty-six-foot Watkins sloop, which was moored near the front door of the Watermans Crab House in Rock Hall. The plan was to sail out into the bay and then to the quiet waters of Swan Cove, a favorite anchorage of the Einsteins.

I arrived a bit early, but my motivation wasn't necessarily the need to be punctual. Instead, I took a table at the Watermans Crab House, and prior to setting sail had a bowl of Maryland crab soup and a tall glass of sweet tea. The Rock Hall version of crab soup is based upon vegetables, a tomato base, and bold chunks of blue crab lurking amid the garden produce. There's a little hint of the flavor of steamed crabs in there, with just enough heat to leave a little glow and make that sweet tea taste awfully good.

It was a great prelude to a sailing trip. I felt satisfied without being sodden, experiencing the Chesapeake Bay with multiple senses: the flavor of spicy crab, the aroma of steaming seafood, the bite of salty air from the nearby bay, the sight of sails going up, the boat slowly picking up speed, the sound of wind filling the sail, laughing gulls howling like hyenas along the crab docks.

Mark and Suzanne have been introducing people to the pleasures of sailing the upper bay for years through their company Blue Crab Chesapeake Charters. Their sloop, appropriately named the *Crab Imperial*, is a sturdy boat, well-fitted, drawing five feet of water. Mark, originally from Baltimore, has sailed all over the bay, to Bermuda and the Caribbean Islands. He has chartered and sailed competitively for more than twenty years. Mark has long hair, a salt and pepper beard, and possibly could have been the subject of a Jimmy Buffet song. Suzanne is the pretty one. She is also from Baltimore and has dark hair, a deep tan, and makes a mean margarita.

Suzanne got the diesel humming and backed the *Crab Imperial* away from its slip while Mark handled the dock lines. Once out of the anchorage, Mark hoisted the sails and we were underway; then he cut the engine and let the sails do their work. When the engine died, so did the conversation. All of us seemed to notice at once the pervasive quiet, the wrinkle of wind in sail, the hiss of the bow cutting through a slight chop. We were moving quickly, quietly, although the breeze was gentle, the boat listing slightly as Mark tightened down on the mainsail.

Mark and Suzanne seem to enjoy sharing their boat, and the bay, with visitors. "We started doing dinner tours in Annapolis in 1994," said Mark. "We'd pick people up at the pier, go sailing, and then take them to a crab house for dinner. Then we decided to come over here. Rock Hall is a small town with roots in commercial fishing, but tourism is becoming a major business. It's a nice blend of the traditional and the innovative, all at the same time. This is a real yachting town, sort of like having Annapolis on the Eastern Shore."

The Einsteins seem to feel at home in this friendly waterfront town. Rock Hall was preparing to celebrate its 300th birthday with a parade and a party, and Mark and Suzanne were working on a float with a sailboat, fittingly, as its theme.

"We've taken out all kinds of people," said Mark. "We've had sailing nuns, and we've had nudists, although not on the same trip. People have gotten engaged on the boat. We've taken couples to Swan Cove, anchored the boat, left them for the night, and returned in the morning with breakfast for them. Whatever people want to do..."

We sailed into the bay briefly, past the community of Gratitude with its lineup of sailing yachts, and then into Swan Cove, one of those quiet, tree-lined anchorages that is becoming more and more rare on the bay. "You sail into a place like this, and you get a feeling for what the bay might have been like years ago," said Mark. Ospreys soared overhead, some taking a meal back to young ones still in the nest. At the head of the cove, a mist settled over the loblolly pines and we moved along silently, pushed by the breeze, realizing that the important thing about a trip is not always arriving at a destination, but embarking on the journey itself.

14

Kent Island

Living Life Before the Bridge

Millions of travelers drive through Kent Island each year, but the average amount of time they spend there could be measured in minutes. Kent Island serves as the eastern approach to the Chesapeake Bay Bridge, the last few miles of Delmarva soil before crossing the high-rise bridge and heading off into the great unknown of Severna Park and Anne Arundel County.

A lot of people say that they've been to Kent Island, but if all they've done is drive through on the way to the bridge, that's sort of like saying they've visited Baltimore because they once flew into BWI Airport. You have to get off the freeway and take to the back roads to really see Kent Island.

I spent a day with two people who know Kent Island and Queen Anne's County as well as anyone, and we seldom cast a shadow on the pavement of U.S. Route 50/301. I was with Nancy Cook, a retired Queen Anne's County schoolteacher, and Judy Edelheit, who works with the Queen Anne's County Office of Tourism. Nancy is from Staunton in the Valley of Virginia, but she moved to Queen Anne's as a young teacher and has been there since. She has a passion for the history of the county, and especially Kent Island, where she taught for many years. Judy was born and raised in Queen Anne's, the daughter of a farmer and waterman who takes great pride in her ancestral ties to the land and water that sustained her family for generations. Judy was Nancy's student at Stevensville High School in the early 1960s.

We set out to see Kent Island as it might have been before the bridge opened for traffic on July 30, 1952. The bridge, also known as the William Preston Lane, Jr. Memorial Bridge, was a miraculous feat of engineering back then; that original two-lane span cost $45 million to build and at the time was the longest continuous over-water steel structure in the world. It was joined by a second span in 1973. Between the two of them, they brought permanent changes to the way of life in Queen Anne's County and Kent Island in particular.

"You have to remember, back then Kent Island was a rural, remote place where people worked on the water and grew crops for the market," said Nancy. "Their lives were very much tied to the bay and to the land that joined it. And it had been that way for hundreds of years, dating back to the times of the Native Americans and to the first English settlement in 1631 by William Claiborne."

Judy was born into that lifestyle. Her father, James Melvin, better known as Hawke, ran a Chesapeake Bay deadrise workboat, catching oysters during the fall and winter, crabs and fish during the summer. If he wasn't on the water, he was working the small family farm, growing crops such as potatoes and green vegetables, to send to the market or to the many canneries that called Queen Anne's home. "It was a wonderful way of life," says Judy. "We have so many natural gifts here — the water, the fertile land — it was wonderful that my mother and father could raise a family that way, living off the land and the water."

We began at the Chesapeake Exploration Center, at 425 Piney Narrows Road, in Chester. The center is just west of Kent Narrows, which separates Kent Island from the mainland Eastern Shore, and it is the headquarters for the county office of tourism. You can pick up maps and brochures here, but the most important thing is the adjoining museum called "Our Chesapeake Legacy." The displays of this small museum are set up to resemble an old country store, and it interprets life along the Chesapeake Bay here from the time of the early Native Americans to the days of tobacco farming. It covers the traditions of working on the water, vegetable farming, transportation, and many other elements of early life in Queen Anne's. It's the perfect place to begin a tour of Kent Island.

From there, we got into the car and hit the back roads. Before the bridge, there were the ferries, which ended their run on the evening of July 30, 1952, the day the bridge opened. First stop was Stevensville, a town that developed around 1850, prospering from the steamboat traffic that linked the eastern and western shores of the Chesapeake in the mid-nineteenth century. The railroad came to Stevensville in 1902, and by 1909 this transportation hub had two schools, four doctors, a blacksmith, and a sawmill.

The town's fortunes declined with the railroad, which ended passenger service in 1938 and freight service ten years later. Today, Stevensville retains its 1920s-era appearance, and was placed on the National Register of Historic Places in 1986. Among the historic buildings are the 1880 Christ Church and 1852 Rectory, which pre-dates the church, and the Cray House, the oldest in Stevensville, which dates from around 1809.

From Stevensville, we headed north on Maryland Route 18, driving through a narrow finger of land that separates the Chesapeake Bay and the Chester River. The road comes to an end at Love Point, which offers a great view of the bay, and then we headed south on state Route 8, driving about seventeen miles to the very southern tip of the island. We stopped in at Matapeake State Park, site of the old ferry terminal, visited historic Kent Manor Inn and Restaurant, and continued on to Romancoke, which is on Eastern Bay, and then all the way south past Bloody Point Creek to Kent Point.

The landscape here is dominated by water. Small creeks thread their way into the upland, and broad, shallow bays reach to the horizon. It's easy to see how Kent Island's proximity to water has dominated its history and culture for centuries. While the bridge has been the catalyst for major changes in Kent Island and Queen Anne's County, you can get on these back roads and explore farmland and creekshore and get an idea of what life might have been like here a half-century or more ago. Even today, deadrise workboats are moored at Kent Island marinas, ready for a trip out to Crab Alley Bay and a day working the water. Times have changed here, but they haven't changed completely.

Queen Anne's Cross Island Trail

Delmarva's Most Diverse Bike Ride

To paraphrase an old saying about the weather, if you don't like the scenery on Queen Anne's County's Cross Island Trail, pedal around the next bend and it will change. This ride, about twelve miles round-trip, is probably the most diverse on Delmarva. It has a little bit of everything, from shopping centers to wild natural areas with spectacular views.

I began a bike ride there at Kent Narrows, parking at the Chesapeake Exploration Center, a multi-faceted building that serves as, among other things, the headquarters of the office of tourism and a museum interpreting life in Queen Anne's County prior to construction of the Chesapeake Bay Bridge. The trail begins at a marina and boatyard, crosses over to a shopping center before quickly disappearing into the woods, and then crosses a salt marsh via a narrow wooden bridge.

Within a minute or so, I went from a busy commercial area to a parking lot to a wooded setting with a great view of a tidal creek flowing under the bridge, minnows schooling in the shallow water, deer and raccoon tracks along the muddy bank. Not exactly a wilderness experience, but a surprise, given the extent of development along the Route 50/301 corridor approaching the bridge. Still, the hum of traffic could be heard over the breeze swaying the tops of the pine trees.

I pedaled on, heading west toward the bridge, and the trail made a sharp right turn and the rumble of traffic became silent. I crossed more wooden bridges, stopping to enjoy the view, and crossed several suburban streets, some of which were under construction. The trail then took on a decidedly rural look, with pines and large hardwood trees growing in thickets along the edge.

Beyond one thicket I heard a loud rumble and the clatter of machinery and saw a cloud of dust rising in the distance. I stopped the bike, got off, and went into the woods to investigate. A farm truck was parked nearby, its cab a faded red and pockmarked with rust. In the field beyond, a gleaning machine was at work harvesting soybeans, which it periodically dumped into the back of the truck. On the other side of the trail, I saw

an old combine in the woods' edge, long ago abandoned, vines and saplings growing up through rusted metal...so, in an instant, not far from the hustle of Route 50 traffic, here was a vivid reminder of Kent Island's agrarian past.

I continued toward the bridge, finding a trail spur on my left with a sign I'd never seen on a bike trail before. "Kent Island Public Library," it read. That's good, I thought, shows that people here have their priorities straight. Bicycles and books, an unbeatable combination.

A playground appeared on my right. I crossed a busy street, and then found myself pedaling through the campus of Kent Island High School, alongside the third-base line of the baseball field. It was then back into the woods, once in a while passing near industrial or commercial buildings that were part of Chesapeake Bay Business Park.

The main part of Cross Island Trail ends here, in a paved parking lot just off Skipjack Parkway, but the cross island experience doesn't end when the asphalt does. Across the parking area is Terrapin Nature Park, a real Kent Island jewel. A narrow trail of crushed shell and gravel runs through the woods, providing access to an open meadow and wetland, with a farm road encircling the open field. This is a great place to look for wildflowers and butterflies in the spring and summer, and it's a good place for birding almost anytime. At the very tip of Kent Island, this park offers a spectacular view of the Chesapeake Bay and the bay bridge carrying traffic to and from the western shore in the distance.

A short spur leaves the main trail and goes down to the beach, providing access to the sandy shore of the bay, and a reminder of the reason Terrapin Nature Park is so-named. In early summer, female diamondback terrapins come ashore under cover of darkness, climb the gentle berm to above the high-tide line, and lay a clutch of eggs in a sandy depression. If they go unnoticed by numerous predators, those eggs will hatch in sixty to one hundred days and young terrapins, about an inch long, will clamber down the beach and into the gentle chop of the bay.

It is a cycle that has been repeated here for centuries, before the bay bridge was built, before the fishing communities of Kent Island were founded, even before William Claiborne settled on the island in 1631. The Native Americans knew terrapins well. Terrapins were an integral part of their diet, and they gave them the name we continue to use today. Terrapin, in the Algonquian language, means "edible turtle."

16

Chesapeake Bay Environmental Center

Leave the Highway Behind and Spend a Day in the Marsh

Delmarva is one of the most misunderstood regions on the Atlantic Coast. People travel through on Route 50, Route 13, or Route 1, and all they see are fast-food restaurants, car dealerships, motels, shopping strips, convenience stores, and all sorts of commercial clutter. Most people are headed to the beach, or they're traveling through to reach points north and south. Delmarva is rarely a destination, but rather more often a means of getting from one place to another.

Through-travelers sometimes come away with a negative opinion. They recall the highway congestion, the proliferation of traffic signals, the ubiquitous fast-food restaurants, the harried memories of having to put up with all of this in order to get where they were going. They rarely see the true essence of Delmarva. They need to take a deep breath, slow down, and get off the main highway...only then will they discover what Delmarva has to offer.

I can think of no better example of this than the Route 50/301 corridor on Kent Island, just east of the Bay Bridge. This area has undergone tremendous commercial development, taking advantage of the millions of travelers each year moving between the D.C. capital area and resort beaches on the ocean or along the bay. If you take an exit and get on a back road, however, you can be in a different environment within minutes. One suggestion: get off at Grasonville at Exit 41, take the Main Street through town, pass the condos and marinas, hang a right on Perry's Corner Road, and in a short distance you'll see a sign for the Chesapeake Bay Environmental Center. Take this dirt lane through the woods and you'll soon cross a salt marsh with a spectacular view in almost all directions. The grassy meadow extends for miles, broken only by little pine and myrtle islands called hummocks, or hammocks, if you prefer. This is typical Chesapeake Country landscape — vast tidal marshes, low islands, and a mix of grasses that slow-dance in the breeze. On the horizon to the north is a narrow strip of buildings; these would be the condos and hotels along Route 50/301, and from here in the marsh they look out of place but unimposing, a benign blot on the landscape from this remote perspective.

The Chesapeake Bay Environmental Center (CBEC) is a preserve of 510 acres, which includes a freshwater impoundment for waterfowl, four miles of hiking trails, a canoe trail, observation towers, photography blinds, and an education center and demonstration gardens. The preserve was begun in 1981 when the Wildfowl Trust of North America bought 315 acres as a sanctuary for migrating waterfowl. It was then named the Horsehead Wetlands Center. The name was changed in 2002 as the preserve grew and emphasis was placed on educating the public about the unique natural environment of the Chesapeake Bay, in particular the wetlands associated with the estuary and the wildlife they support.

Today, the center plays an active role in educating school groups and adults, and training programs are held for federal and state personnel, civic organizations, and private landowners. In addition to serving as a campus to enlighten people about the natural system of the bay and its wetlands, the center has played an active role in bay restoration. The center created a CBEC Restoration Volunteer Corps in 2004, and since then has worked with partners to construct four oyster reefs, plant seven million oyster spat, and establish hundreds of acres of wetlands grasses.

For the casual visitor, the center is a great place to learn about the ecology of the bay and to experience firsthand the wetlands, streams, ponds, and woodlands that are part of the landscape of the estuary. The visitor and education center would be a good place to begin. Take the causeway across the wetlands and you'll enter a parking area adjacent to the visitor center, where demonstration gardens and various other exhibits are located. You can pick up a map here showing the ten hiking trails on the preserve, some of which are short walks, others longer, but all with interesting things to see.

Trails begin at the parking area and a picnic pavilion is located here as well. A short trail circles the perimeter of a hummock, providing a close-up look at these phenomena of the wetlands landscape. Hummocks are slightly higher than the surrounding marsh and support vegetation more often found in an upland environment. There are loblolly pines, holly, wax myrtle, greenbrier, and various other forest species. These little islands provide cover and food for animals, nesting birds, and other wildlife.

An adjacent trail runs along the edge of Marshy Creek, with the freshwater impoundment on the opposite side. In the winter, dabbling ducks can be seen on the pond, and blinds provide a great viewing spot. Near the tip of the peninsula is a raised platform, providing a look at Marshy Creek and Route 50 in the distance. In the fall, rafts of hundreds of ruddy ducks gather here. Other trails circle the impoundment, run through meadows and reforested areas, and along a small beach.

When you're driving through on Route 50/301, it's easy to get the notion that the landscape is dominated by commercial development, but spend some time at the environmental center and you will begin to see what the real Kent Island is like. There are thousands of acres of wild wetlands dotted with ponds, hummocks, and shallow bays. In addition to ducks gathering in the fall and winter, bald eagles come here to nest in January. It's a wonderful landscape to discover — all you have to do is take the freeway exit.

17

Wye Island

Wild Times on the Wye River

You never know what you're going to come across at Wye Island Natural Resources Management Area in Queen Anne's County. On a Sunday in late November, I was walking around a cut-over cornfield, enjoying the last of the fall colors, when I saw a pair of bobwhite quail on the ground in front of me. It's not uncommon to see quail at Wye Island, but these two were a lot more nonchalant than quail should be. They were foraging for seeds along the grassy edge of the field, paying me no mind as I approached to within six feet of them.

I skirted around the feeding birds, and moments later a handsome pointer came around the bend, nose to the ground, radio collar around its neck. And then came about twenty-five men and women on horseback, following the lone bird dog. The pointer, searching for quail, looked up and saw me and was obviously surprised and confused, unsure of what to do next. Its handler, leading the pack of riders, shouted, "Leave it!", and the dog quickly retreated and resumed the hunt.

I had inadvertently stumbled into one of the Wye Island bird-dog field trials, held several times each year on the state-owned farm. The quail were pen-raised birds, planted as quarry for the bird dogs, which explains their lack of fear of humans.

Wye Island is a beautiful place, managed for wildlife by the Maryland Department of Natural Resources. Of the island's 2,800 acres, 2,450 are in agriculture, mainly grain crops such as corn and soybeans. Visiting this natural area is like stepping back in time. Once you're in the farming area, the roads are dirt, and the fields are separated by wide hedgerows, home to all kinds of wildlife. You could be on a central Georgia quail plantation, except that most of the fields and trails have great waterfront views.

You reach Wye Island by taking Carmichael Road off Route 50 near Chesapeake College. It's a good bet that millions of people have driven past Carmichael Road on their way to the beach resorts without realizing what a treasure lies at the end of this two-lane blacktop. Carmichael Road passes through forests and farm fields, a few residential areas, and then crosses Wye Narrows via an old wooden bridge. Cross the bridge, and you're on Wye Island, separated from the mainland by the Wye River and the Wye East River.

I went to Wye Island for the trails, not the quail, and this place has some great ones. As you drive onto the natural resource management area, the paved road veers to the left and ends at a small conference center called the Duck House, formerly a hunting lodge. The managed area begins just past the Duck House, along Wye Island Road, a dirt and gravel road that runs some four miles across the island. Six miles of hiking trails branch off Wye Island Road, providing a look at an old growth forest, a sheltered cove, and a giant holly tree estimated to be more than 275 years old.

My favorite is Ferry Landing Trail, a narrow lane that once provided access to a hand-drawn ferry running to Bennett's Point on the other side of the Wye River. The trail runs through what amounts to be a huge hedgerow separating two farm fields. The trees are mostly old hardwoods, many of them leaning across the path, creating a canopy overhead. The trail has numerous Osage orange trees, and in the fall their lime-green fruits are scattered along the path.

The trail veers to the right, and the open water can be seen in the distance, but another short trail, called Jack-in-the-Pulpit, branches off, circling through the woods and back to the sandy beach where the ferry once landed. This trail passes through a thicket of Osage, various other hardwoods, and huge wild grapevines, some of which actually form a roof overhead, making the trail enclosed by vegetation.

The longest trail is Dividing Creek, a two-and-a-half-mile walk along farm fields and hedgerows, a good place for birding. Schoolhouse Woods Trail and Holly Tree Loop provide a look at an old growth forest with towering hardwoods, as well as the ancient holly that stands on the edge of a farm field a few hundred yards off Wye Island Road. Osage Trail is a loop of about a half-mile that passes along Big Woods Cove, a good place to see waterfowl in the winter.

Most of the trails are intended for foot travel only, but bicyclists would enjoy riding on Wye Island Road, as long as the weather hasn't been too dry, in which case dust could make riding uncomfortable.

Wye Island has been used by the state as a natural resources management area since the mid-1970s. Today, the tradition of agricultural use continues, so for more than three hundred years the fields of Wye Island have produced tobacco, wheat, corn, soybeans, and much more.

In the 1700s the island was owned by two men, William Paca, the third governor of Maryland and a signer of the Declaration of Independence, and Charles Beale Bordley, a prominent lawyer and jurist. Dividing Creek separated the two men's parcels, with Paca owning the northern portion and Bordley the southern. Bordley gave up his law practice to live full-time on Wye Island, attempting to create a totally self-sufficient farming community. He built a winery, a brick-yard, planted an orchard, made textiles, and even operated his own brewery.

It's a good bet that he also had a good bird dog or two and enjoyed working the hedgerows where his corn and wheat grew. On Wye Island, it's good to see that traditions such as these are passed along.

18

Oxford Country

Quintessential Maryland Eastern Shore

It was early winter and I was driving on Route 333 from Easton to Oxford. It had rained earlier, but the clouds were breaking up and now and then the sun would shine through, casting slivers of golden light on cut-over cornfields. Flocks of Canada geese were flying in ragged strings over pine woods and hedgerows, setting their wings, coasting, balancing on the wind, and finally dropping into damp fields to feed.

I put down the window and listened. Canada geese are ubiquitous on the Eastern Shore, considered pests by folks who run golf courses, but on a brilliant day in early winter, when they're coasting into a rural cornfield, singing all the while, they seem to symbolize the essence of the Eastern Shore.

Driving past rural farms, past long driveways threading back through tall oaks, it occurred to me that this stretch of two-lane highway shows the Eastern Shore as we like to think of it. There is no bustling traffic, no crowds, no shopping malls. What we have is open space, wild birds, and country lanes that end at the water's edge. It is a verdant land, peaceful.

I had not been in Oxford in years. It's not a place you pass through on the way to somewhere else. You have to want to go there, and I did. We all need to get a little of Oxford now and then. The town of Oxford lies at the very end of Oxford Neck, forming the south side of the mouth of the Tred Avon River. For the uninitiated, along the Chesapeake, the term "neck" is used to describe a finger of high land separated from other necks by a body of water. In other localities, necks might be called peninsulas, but we call them necks, and they usually come in multiple numbers.

Leaving Easton on Route 333 (Oxford Road), I drove across Edmundson Neck, crossed Peachblossom Creek onto Bailey's Neck, and then crossed Trippe Creek to Oxford Neck. South of Oxford Neck are Island Creek and Island Neck and La Trappe Creek and Grubin Neck.

These rural necks are great places to explore, and one of the best drives on Delmarva is a loop that includes Easton, Oxford, a ferry ride across the Tred Avon, and a look at lush countryside and small towns whose pulse is tied to the push-and-pull of the tides.

I drove from Easton to Oxford, took the ferry over to Bellevue, and then drove on to Royal Oak, where I took Route 329 to Route 33, the link between Easton, St. Michaels, and Tilghman Island. From there, it was back to where I began, completing the loop. It's not a long drive, perhaps twenty-five miles. It occurred to me that it would be a great bicycle loop. The secondary roads are wide, there is little traffic except in the immediate Easton area, and this ride is rich in sensory elements: fresh air to breathe, goose music to enjoy, and frequently the sight of interesting old homes or waterfront coves well removed from the tourist traffic.

The town of Oxford, of course, is the star. It could be a movie set with its neat old cottages set close together, narrow streets, brick walkways, huge shade trees, and always the water. There are yacht yards and marinas, quiet coves, small creeks to explore, and special places, such as the Robert Morris Inn, which offers fine food and accommodations on the banks of the Tred Avon, just up the street from the ferry terminal.

Whether you drive or take the bike to Oxford, the best way to explore the town is by foot. Oxford is one of the oldest towns in Maryland, officially chartered in 1694, and was one of the original ports of entry for British vessels in Colonial times. A replica of the first custom house is at the ferry landing, and the ferry itself is believed to be the oldest private ferry in operation in the United States. It began in 1683.

A walking tour of Oxford will give you a close look at the history of this area of Chesapeake Bay country. Many of the cottages in town were built in the eighteenth century and the town still has the feel of "living" history — that is, its history has not been exploited for commercial reasons, but is simply there for visitors to discover.

Route 33 literally comes to a dead-end on the banks of the Tred Avon River in downtown Oxford. Find a place to park and explore from here. Several blocks of old homes lie off Morris Street and Strand Road, and there is a public park on Morris Street that offers picnic tables and a great view of the river. Marinas and yacht yards abound, with numerous well-appointed pleasure boats ready to head into the Chesapeake. Cutts & Case, world-renowned for yacht design and construction, is on Tilghman Street.

If you've worked up a powerful hunger, there are inns, taverns, bistros, and numerous other places to get everything from a sandwich to a gourmet meal. When the novelist James Michener was in the area writing *Chesapeake*, he stayed at the Robert Morris Inn and declared their crab cakes the best. I can't attest to that, but I'm more than willing to do the research to corroborate his findings.

19

Adkins Arboretum

Native Plants are Just the Beginning

Lynn and I were hiking a woodland trail at Adkins Arboretum when we spotted a little man peering out from a hole at the base of an oak tree. We had been following a bird that was skipping along the trail in front of us, refusing to fly, but never allowing us to get closer than six feet. Lynn looked at it with the binoculars and identified it as an ovenbird; it had pink legs and an orange stripe along the head.

The ovenbird led us to the little man, who was in a hollow about eight inches wide at the base of the tree. The little man had sticks for arms, a clay head, stringy hair, and bulging eyes. He didn't have much to say.

Turns out the little man was the creation of an artist from Adelphi, Maryland, named Gary Irby, who, along with a half-dozen other artists from around the country, had turned four hundred acres of forest and meadow into a giant sculpture garden, where a walk in the woods is filled with surprises.

Adkins Arboretum is near Ridgely, a few miles northeast of Easton. The arboretum is in Tuckahoe State Park, through which runs the Tuckahoe River. It is a rural setting, with fields, forests, and only a few farmhouses scattered around the landscape.

Adkins Arboretum is one of our favorite places to hike and watch birds. Four miles of trails wind through hardwood forest, swamp, and meadow, and given that the arboretum's mission is the propagation of native plants and wildflowers, the setting is spectacular in most seasons. On a recent visit, the outdoor sculptures were an added bonus. Each summer a new exhibit goes up, sometimes with artists solicited by invitation nationwide; other times the works are provided by local artisans, such as Howard and Mary McCoy of Centreville.

Before Lynn and I began our hike, we stopped by the visitor center and said hello to Ellie Altman, executive director of the arboretum, who told us that the area we were about to explore had narrowly escaped becoming lake bottom. "When Tuckahoe State Park was created, the plan was to flood this area and create a swimming reservoir," Altman said, "but there was a giant oak tree on the property, and local residents wanted to save the tree, so the plan to flood the area was dropped and the idea of an arboretum arose from the effort to save the oak."

The arboretum opened in 1980 as part of the state park, but it was not until 1998, when a non-profit organization was formed, that the day-to-day operation of the arboretum became independent. "A nearby landowner who was very interested in native plants bequeathed a significant amount of money to operate the arboretum," explained Altman. "This endowment and member donations provide our operating capital today. We have a small staff and a very large group of volunteers who are very dedicated."

The mission of the arboretum is the propagation of native plants and to teach people how to be good stewards of the land. Altman further explained that it is part of the Chesapeake Bay watershed. "So what we do here on the land directly affects the quality of the bay...We try to make that point to people who visit us here," she said.

Indeed, to reach the visitor center, one must park the car and walk across a footbridge that spans a freshwater marsh that includes dozens of native plants. "When we opened, the marsh was an open pond that had been dug years ago, so we re-filled it and created a wetland," said Altman.

The boardwalk leads to a small interpretive center where information on the arboretum and park can be obtained. There also is a meeting room where exhibits are held, a gift shop, and restrooms. The trails begin just outside the back door.

Lynn and I walked along a meadow and then turned right into a wooded area where one of the first sculptures was located. It was a trio of stone sculptures by Barbara Josephs Liotta called *Three Graces*. Across the way, in the meadow, mowed paths led to an egg-shaped "blind" made of black cherry twigs salvaged from the arboretum's brush pile. Knox Cummings, a Vermont artist, calls his work *Meadow Arcs*.

We walked along a stream that meanders through a hardwood forest, finding various surprises on our way: blue and silver spheres suspended in a woodland glade, stick figures watching us from off the trail, rocks suspended by wooden tripods, and bundles of grasses and twigs woven into delicate patterns.

We followed the woodland trail downhill to a stream — nearly dry in the hot weather — and then climbed back to the meadow, circled a field of blooming wildflowers, and made our way back to the visitor center. Along the way, we saw dozens of trees and plants native to this coastal habitat. We could easily identify some, but others required reference to the trail guide supplied by the arboretum. Many trees and plants are identified by discreetly placed signs, large enough to be helpful, but small enough to preserve the "wild" feeling of the landscape.

While we have enjoyed walks through the arboretum in the past, the addition of outdoor sculpture within the landscape adds a surprising new dimension. Most of the pieces are made of materials found on-site, so they complement the woodland setting, creating an interesting combination of the artist's eye and the natural landscape.

One of the arboretum's favorite activities is the twice-yearly plant sale, held in May, on the Saturday before Mothers Day, and in the fall, the weekend after Labor Day. This is a major fund-raiser for the arboretum, and it also provides an opportunity for gardeners to buy plants they know are native to the Delmarva Peninsula and to the coastal plain. According to the arboretum, the sale includes more than 250 species of wildflowers, grasses, vines, shrubs, and trees, many propagated at the arboretum nursery from locally collected seed.

The propagation of native plants is truly the mission of the arboretum. Unlike some larger public botanic gardens that boast collections of thousands of species from around the world, Adkins knows its niche is Delmarva and the watershed of the Chesapeake Bay. "The native plants of the Delmarva Peninsula have evolved together with insects, birds, mammals, and other wildlife since the last Ice Age, 10,000 years ago," said Ellie. "They are part of a complex natural system, an ecosystem, and are adapted to this region's climate, rainfall, and soils. These plants belong here."

20

Chesapeake Bay Maritime Museum

At St. Michaels, It's All About Boats

I can think of few museums that allow visiting children to run roughshod over displays, but at the Chesapeake Bay Maritime Museum in St. Michaels, such behavior is not only allowed, but encouraged. On a visit not long ago, just before the end of the school year, dozens of fifth graders were on a field trip. They swarmed over the Hooper Strait Lighthouse, climbed through a model Chesapeake Bay skipjack, and searched for blue crabs that might be swimming beneath the dock. In general, they had a fine old time. I had the feeling that this trip might be memorable for them. There was much smiling and laughter, precious few personal electronic devices.

The Chesapeake Bay Maritime Museum contradicts the usual perception of what a museum should be. This is not a place of dusty artifacts lodged in a shadowy building with uniformed guards giving you the eye. Indeed, most of our time at the museum is spent outdoors, walking.

The museum more closely resembles a campus than an archive. It is spread over eighteen acres of waterfront, with many restored buildings, boat warehouses, shops, and galleries. The 1879 lighthouse, which once guided mariners through Hooper Strait, is a focal point of the museum grounds. The bandstand that once echoed with Glen Miller tunes at Tolchester Beach is nearby. Other buildings explore the role the bay has played in American history, in the waterfowl hunting tradition of the Chesapeake, and in the economic ebb and flow of Chesapeake Bay communities and families.

This is an active museum, where in warm weather you can watch watermen sort their catch, take sailing lessons, or learn to build your own boat or carve a hunting decoy. Restoration is an on-going process at St. Michaels. Historic buildings are being renovated, and a large shed houses old boats in various stages of repair. Visitors are encouraged to watch and ask questions. Indeed, apprentices are enlisted to help build cedar lapstrake skiffs, which are, in turn, sold to raise funds for the museum.

M. A. CLARKE

Traditional Chesapeake Bay skipjacks once worked the bay by the hundreds, but only a handful of these sail-powered oyster dredges still exist. Visitors can see the *Caleb W. Jones*, a beautiful skipjack built in Reedville in 1953, docked next door to the Hooper Strait Lighthouse. A more thorough look at oystering can be had in the "Oystering on the Chesapeake" building, which includes an oyster dredgeboat visitors are encouraged to climb aboard and explore. The building traces the economic impact of oysters around the Chesapeake Bay region, including how they were caught, packaged, and marketed.

The Small Boat Shed is a waterfront warehouse that houses the nation's largest collection of Chesapeake Bay watercraft. Most of these small boats were designed for working the bay, for catching crabs in shallow grass beds, for tonging oysters, or for fishing. One example, the Choptank River shad skiff, was built in the 1930s as a sailing skiff, and was later converted to inboard and outboard power. These boats are wonderful examples of the dictum "form follows function." The function of most of these boats was to harvest seafood, and they were built with this in mind. Boats intended for collecting soft crabs in shallow water, for example, had flat bottoms to allow them to navigate water a foot or less in depth.

The Steamboat Building is one of the largest on the grounds. It explores the role mechanical power played in shaping the lives of those who worked and played on the bay, and there are many artifacts from the steam era, including the dramatic photograph of the *City of Norfolk* making her way into Baltimore Harbor in 1961.

The newest building is called "At Play on the Bay," and it emphasizes the recreational aspects of boating rather than seafood harvesting and transportation. On display are pleasure craft, such as an early Owens cabin cruiser, a log canoe, and many examples of sport-fishing memorabilia.

The maritime museum experience is not limited to the eighteen-acre campus, however. Tour boats leave the grounds four times a day, taking passengers on a narrated cruise of the Miles River. It's a great way to learn about the colorful history of St. Michaels, to see historic riverfront homes, to view wildlife, and to watch watermen harvest clams, oysters, and crabs, depending upon the season. Cruises last an hour to an hour-and-a-half and are available from March through November.

21

Pickering Creek Audubon Center

Talbot County's Campus for Environmental Education

Easton is one of our family's favorite places to visit, especially in the fall when the hardwoods show color, the geese are in the cornfields, and it's time to break out the winter woolies. Easton has a long tradition of waterfowl hunting, celebrated each November by the famous Wildfowl Festival, a carnival of wildlife art, antique decoys, duck-calling competitions, retriever demonstrations, and a myriad of other things having to do with the culture of the hunt.

Even if you're not a hunter, the Easton area is a pleasant place to be, especially once you leave behind the traffic and clutter of U.S. Route 50 and take to the back roads. Easton is like many towns on Delmarva; you don't see the best side when passing through on busy thoroughfares such as Route 50, Route 13, or Route 113. Hie thee to the back roads.

Easton, of course, has a lovely downtown, just a few blocks away from Route 50. There are restaurants, shops, galleries, and the stately Tidewater Inn, and if you visit during the Wildfowl Festival, the town will be bursting with arts and crafts with an outdoor theme.

A few miles outside of town is another favorite place, Pickering Creek Audubon Center, a four-hundred-acre preserve of farmland, forest, meadow, and tidal creeks. One of the initial pleasures of Pickering Creek is the simple matter of getting there. Once you exit the Easton town limits, Talbot County is emphatically rural, with neat farms, woodlands, and an abundance of open space. Maryland has a wonderful system of secondary roads that make traveling on the back roads a pleasure. The roadways are wide, well-maintained, and amazingly free of litter, exemplified by those leading out to Pickering Creek.

Traveling west on Route 50, turn left at Airport Road in Easton and then immediately turn right onto Route 622 (Longwoods Road). Follow Route 622 to Sharp Road, turn left, and the center will be on your right. The Pickering Creek center is operated by the Chesapeake Audubon Society and includes woodland, upland, and wetlands. It has long been a working farm, and though the property was donated to Audubon a number of years ago, 270 acres are still under production. The farm, with a mile of shoreline on a tidal creek, was donated by Margaret Strahl and her brother, George Olds, in 1984. The family's wish was that the property be accessible to all members of the community, and the center is open today, free of charge, from sunrise to sunset, 365 days a year.

While the fields at Pickering still produce crops, the mission today is environmental education. The center has become a leader in this regard, with 16,000 school children visiting each year to learn about the Chesapeake Bay watershed and how best to protect it.

We go to Pickering Creek for the birding, which means abundant waterfowl in the fall and many colorful songbirds during the migration in the spring. There are open fields, meadows, hardwood swamps, shoreline, open water, freshwater ponds... just about any habitat you can think of, all of which means a great diversity of birds.

A hiking trail covers a wide variety of habitat and offers especially good birding in the spring and fall. The head of the trail is near the center office, which once was the family homestead. A mixed hardwood forest at the beginning of the trail is prime songbird habitat. A variety of woodpeckers also live in the woods, as do barred and great-horned owls. Look for rufous-sided towhees in the undergrowth.

The trail crosses several bogs and winds along the banks of the creek, where waterfowl and wading birds can be seen. It ends at the farm equipment sheds, where an organic demonstration garden is maintained.

We usually walk back to the trail head along the gravel road, where, often, there are hawks hunting over the cornfields and bluebirds along the field edges. In the fall, great numbers of yellow-rumped warblers can be seen in this edge habitat where farm field, shrub, and forest meet.

One of the best birding spots is the bus parking lot, which is along the field edge just as the road enters the woods near the office building. The sun is at your back during most daylight hours here, making it easier to see detail and color. There is a large walnut tree along the edge, along with numerous plants and shrubs preferred by birds. Ruby-crowned kinglets are plentiful in these shrubs in fall.

Pickering Creek offers many programs for students and adults during the year. The center has more than 240 volunteers, who do everything from trail maintenance to leading field trips, so whether your interest is birds or botany, the center will likely have programs that will interest you. Indeed, you may have a skill that the center could use and you might want to turn a visit into a volunteer opportunity. It has been known to happen.

22

Tilghman Island

Rock Stars on the 20th Anniversary

When Lynn and I were planning our twentieth wedding anniversary a few years ago, we began looking for a weekend retreat. We weren't sure where we wanted to go, but we knew what we didn't want.

"I don't want to go someplace where they sell Christmas ornaments year-round," said Lynn.

"And I don't want to go to a place that has pink, heart-shaped Jacuzzis," I said.

That narrowed it right down.

So we picked a place that offers everything we enjoy: outdoor sports, wonderful food, and friendly, unpretentious service. We went rock-fishing at Capt. Buddy Harrison's Chesapeake House on Tilghman Island, Maryland.

Truth is, you're not likely to find Tilghman Island on many couples' short list of romantic getaways. Cancun it ain't. This is a working watermen's town, a place where skipjacks still dredge oysters and boats are used for business more often than pleasure. To reach Tilghman Island, you drive to Easton on U.S. Route 50, head west on Maryland Route 33, pass through St. Michaels, and keep driving until the road ends. Welcome to Tilghman Island, where being on the water means work, and that's why we like it.

We like the throaty growl of those diesel-powered deadrises, and we enjoy the dock-side commerce and the unloading of the day's catch of fish, crabs, or oysters. We like to watch those lanky crabhouse cats that belong to no one, but make up their own community. This is an honest and authentic place, an island that so far has escaped gentrification. It is a place of great beauty.

Tilghman Island is a short drive from Easton and St. Michaels, but it is a world apart from these two tourism-oriented towns. Easton straddles the busy Route 50 thoroughfare and is a combination of retail trade and small town charm. The Route 50 corridor is forever expanding, with restaurant and hotel chains, shopping centers, and convenience stores. Easton is also a historic town, though, and once visitors exit Route 50, they find wonderful old homes, interesting shops, restaurants, and a restored downtown with much appeal.

St. Michaels, only a few miles away on Route 33, likewise draws its share of tourists, especially those whose interest is the seafaring tradition of the Eastern Shore. St. Michaels has shops and restaurants, but the real draw is the Chesapeake Bay Maritime Museum, a sprawling, campus-like setting at the downtown harbor.

It is typical of Delmarva that as one becomes further removed from the busy thoroughfares, the pace becomes slower and the culture reflects more of what we consider authentic Eastern Shore. For example, shops and restaurants in Easton and St. Michaels offer upscale goods that might be found in, let's say, Washington and Northern Virginia, but by the time we head out Route 33, all the way to Tilghman, the shops will be offering fish hooks, frozen squid, white bread, and a six-pack of Blue Ribbon. Restaurant fare is not gourmet, but it is plentiful, fresh, simply prepared, delicious, and offered without pretension or inflated price. This is a formula that the Harrison family has used with great success since the days of the steamships.

The Harrisons have operated the Chesapeake House for more than a century. Back during the days of steamships, Capt. Levin Harrison would dock his cargo vessel in Baltimore and local residents would inquire about places along the bay to escape the summer heat of the city. Capt. Harrison's wife, Ida, was a schoolteacher with free time during the summer, so the family began taking in boarders.

In the early days of the business, the guests were mainly women and children, but later the men began coming with their families, and the Harrisons began taking them fishing.

The fifth generation of the Harrison family is now involved in the business, which is presided over by Capt. Levin Harrison III, whom everyone knows simply as Capt. Buddy. Capt. Buddy has a twinkle in his eye and is quick with a story, and he knows his family's success in the hospitality business is built upon generations of happy customers. "We do everything we can to please our guests," he says. "We like to see smiling faces."

Like Tilghman Island, Chesapeake House is honest and unpretentious. The main building is a white, two-story block and frame lodge on the edge of town. The restaurant is attached, and separate guest quarters are located across the lawn. The boat dock is around back.

Guests at Chesapeake House come for two reasons: the food, meaning abundant fresh local seafood; and the fishing, which, depending upon the season, could mean rockfish, bluefish, trout, croakers, flounder, or a mix of the above. A set fee gets you a night's lodging, dinner, breakfast, a fishing trip, and a boxed lunch on the boat.

Dinner is family style and plentiful. On our visit, Capt. Buddy was featuring his popular oyster buffet, which presents oysters prepared in nearly every conceivable manner. We began with a plate of raw ones on the halfshell, opened for us as we waited. We then sampled creamy oyster stew, single fried oysters, oyster fritters, oysters on the halfshell broiled with crab imperial and bacon, and oysters in a Creole sauce with rice.

To add some land-based balance to this seafood feast, there was also fried chicken, ham, lima beans, stewed tomatoes, and homemade biscuits.

Breakfast is equally ample and is served early. We were on the boat before seven and watched the sunrise aboard the *Lady Peggy* with skipper Allen Bryan as we headed into the Chesapeake to an area called Summer Gooses, which had been a hot spot for rockfish, or striped bass, when we were there.

Capt. Allen throttled down the big diesel, turned into the current, and dropped anchor. We would chum and use light spinning rigs, so a sizeable rockfish would be a challenge. I prefer this method to trolling because you can feel the fish the instant it hits, and the light tackle is more sporting.

Capt. Allen used a ladle to spoon out some ground menhaden, which floated off in the current behind us. We then baited up with soft-shell clams and let the baits drift back with the chum. "We're fishing in about thirty feet of water, so we'll put on different size sinkers and fish various depths," said Capt. Allen. "Rockfish feed in the entire water column, so we'll do some experimenting."

The idea is for the chum to attract the fish, which then will take your bait. For the first fifteen minutes or so, the menhaden attracted only gulls, but then Lynn's rod dipped, the drag began singing, and we had engaged our first rockfish of the day.

Capt. Allen leaned over the stern, netted the fish, and measured it. It was a tad under eighteen inches, the legal minimum, so we gently released it. By lunchtime, though, there would be more than two dozen others, some keepers, some not. Lynn caught one just before quitting time that measured more than twenty-three inches, and that one came home with us, and on the following evening, glazed with rosemary butter, it graced our dinner table.

23

Blackwater National Wildlife Refuge

Delmarva's Best Place to See Eagles

Blackwater National Wildlife Refuge, near Cambridge, may be the best place on Delmarva to see bald eagles. Lynn and I go to Blackwater at least once a year because it's a good place to see waterfowl, but on a recent fall visit we saw an even dozen bald eagles in a single afternoon. There were eagles soaring with turkey vultures over the vast marshes. We saw them perched on pine snags and resting on exposed tidal flats. We even saw one dive on a fox in a cornfield near the visitor center.

What makes Blackwater such an eagle magnet? The easy answer is that it has everything an eagle needs: plenty of open space in which to hunt, plentiful food such as fish and small mammals, tall pines to nest in, and an absence of human interference. The area along the Blackwater River south of Cambridge is sparsely populated. It is low country, with farm fields, forests, and vast marshes where muskrats have been trapped for centuries.

When Lynn and I visited, instead of taking the main route (Maryland Route 16) from Cambridge, we turned south in Vienna and made our way along unmarked country roads, crossing wooden, single-lane bridges, and driving along causeways that seemed only slightly higher than sea level. We were rewarded with some spectacular scenery, nearly no traffic, and eagle sightings before we got near the refuge.

Blackwater refuge, at more than 27,000 acres, is vast. Surrounding it are state lands, such as Fishing Bay and Taylor's Island Wildlife Management areas, which add even more to the protected area. This combination of woodland, open water, farm fields, and wetlands is prime habitat for eagles and many other birds. The wildlife refuge was created in 1933 to provide wintering grounds for migrating waterfowl, but, like most refuges of the era, the constituency has grown in recent years to include a varied list of birds and mammals.

Lynn and I began our tour of Blackwater by stopping by the visitor center to pick up trail maps and look at the interpretive displays, which cover the history and natural history of the Blackwater area. The visitor center was recently renovated and enlarged, and a second-floor viewing area provides a great venue for scanning the impoundments with the binoculars. A self-guided wildlife drive begins a short distance past the center, but before getting underway we decided that a walk would give us a chance to stretch the legs and see the refuge up-close.

Marsh Edge Trail, near the entrance of Wildlife Drive, is not long, but it covers a remarkable diversity of habitat. We began in a mature loblolly pine woods, crossed to a transition zone, where marsh meets woodland, skirted the open water of Little Blackwater River, and ended in the pine forest near where we began. It's a great place to see birds other than eagles, herons, and waterfowl. Take things slowly, check the sunlit pine canopy with the binoculars, and you're likely to see nuthatches, chickadees, kinglets, creepers, goldfinches, and a variety of sparrows.

This trail provides a great example of an "edge," or transition zone, where one habitat meets another. As the forest of loblolly pine nears the marsh, the elevation falls slightly and the pines are replaced by plants that can withstand periodic inundation when the Little Blackwater rises. There is wax myrtle, groundsel tree, red cedar, and other shrubs, and as the elevation drops even more, marsh plants such as cattails and three-square bulrushes. This edge habitat is very important to wildlife, providing food, nesting, and protection from predators.

The best place to see waterfowl is along Wildlife Drive, a gravel lane running along an embankment that helped create the freshwater impoundments built for migrating waterfowl. When we last visited, there were numerous Canada geese, mallards, pintails, green-winged teal, shovelers, and tundra swans. Great blue herons patrolled the marsh edges, searching for small fish.

Blackwater is managed with waterfowl in mind, so the impoundments are drained each summer to encourage the germination of seed-producing plants, such as wild millet and smartweed, which provide food for waterfowl. In late summer, the water control structures are closed to allow rainfall to fill the impoundments by the time ducks arrive in early fall. Upland fields are planted in corn and other grains, which are left standing through the winter.

The open water opposite the impoundments was once a vast marsh, but over the years much of the vegetation has been lost. According to refuge records, more than 7,000 acres of marsh have been lost since the refuge was established in 1933. There are numerous reasons for this: a rising sea level, wind and wave erosion, high water salinity during droughts, and changes in the flow of the Blackwater and Little Blackwater Rivers.

Loss of vegetation is also blamed on an invasive mammal called the nutria, which was introduced from South America in the 1930s for use in the fur trade. Nutria, which are larger than native muskrats, have a ravenous appetite for marsh grasses, pulling them up by the root and leaving behind bare soil that is susceptible to erosion. Thousands of nutria occupy the marshes of Blackwater, and state and federal agencies have begun programs to control them.

Wildlife Drive is also probably the best place at Blackwater to see bald eagles. Check out the dead trees, called snags, across the open water, as well as the tall loblolly pines that line the waterfront. These are favorite nesting and roosting spots for eagles, hawks, and vultures. The refuge has more than seventy-five eagles year-round, a number that can double during migration in winter, so, if you want to see eagles, grab the binoculars and spend a winter afternoon on Wildlife Drive at Blackwater. It's the best place on Delmarva to see our national bird.

24

Deal Island

An Honest, Unpretentious Waterman's Town

On a blustery February morning the sign in front of White's Market in St. Stephens advertised a popular winter special: fresh muskrats. White's Market, on Route 363, is on the way to Deal Island, a scenic outpost removed from the Delmarva fast land by some five miles of cordgrass marsh, shallow ponds, and meandering little waterways called guts.

On my way to Deal Island I noticed a battered old car parked on the shoulder, and I slowed, thinking someone might have car trouble. The wind was cutting out of the northwest at twenty to twenty-five, with nothing to stop it but a sea of tattered brown grass. Not a good place for a breakdown...but then I saw a solitary figure wading through the marsh, walking with that helter-skelter gait that comes from sinking calf-deep in muck, pausing between steps to pull the back foot free before swinging it forward. It was a man of some age, thin as cordgrass, and he had a good rhythm going. I knew he had spent many a winter day out there, and his car was not broken down at all. He was carrying steel traps in one hand, and in the other were sticks of bamboo with strips of orange tape. He was setting his trap line, and I wondered whether he might be the source of the White's Market special of the week.

You don't see this much anymore, since the combination of super synthetic materials and political activism by the animal rights movement has made the wearing of animal skins unnecessary and politically incorrect. You also don't see muskrat listed on many big-city restaurant menus.

Not so here on Deal Island. While many waterfront communities along the Chesapeake Bay have gone from working the water to working the tourists —from crab shanties to condos — Deal Island remains an honest, hard-knuckled, working waterman's town, where life still revolves around trapping 'rats in the winter and crab-potting in the summer.

Driving out Deal Island Road is like stepping back in time. Leave U.S. Route 13 in Princess Anne, turn west on Route 363, and, after passing a residential community, you'll see Somerset County as it might have been fifty years ago. There are pine woods and farm fields, the occasional homestead with barns and various other outbuildings, and small communities with intriguing names: St. Stephens, Oriole, Dames Quarter, Monie, and Chance.

After about eight miles, the landscape opens to reveal the Delmarva version of the Great Plains. North and south, as far as the eye can see, lie vast meadows of grass interrupted now and then by little islands of stunted pines and cedars called hummocks, or hammocks. This would be the Deal Island Wildlife Management Area (WMA), a 13,000-acre preserve that is one of the most important waterfowl refuges in the East. More than eighty percent of the WMA is tidal wetland, and it includes a 2,800-acre, man-made impoundment created to provide food and habitat for migratory ducks, geese, and other birds.

Cross this vast sea of grass and you enter the community of Chance, continue across the bridge and you're in Deal Island, with its marina on the right, churches, school, homes, cemeteries, and a few stores. Pass through Deal Island, cross another marsh, and you're in Wenona, where Route 363 comes to an uncelebrated end at the town marina. Deal Island and Wenona are authentic working watermen towns — you won't find fancy restaurants and shops that sell hundred-dollar golf shirts. What you will see, depending upon the season, are Chesapeake Bay deadrise workboats outfitted for crabbing, skipjacks that sail for oysters in the fall and winter, crab shanties where catches of blue crabs are packaged for market, and fishermen heading out to Tangier Sound to try their luck with trout, rockfish, and croakers.

For a small community, Deal Island seems to have an inordinate number of churches, and you soon begin to realize the important role religion plays in this community. Life here is based upon faith: living hand-in-fist with the bay, depending upon nature for your sustenance, trusting that the tide will rise only so far, and then ebb.

The church has long-been central to Deal Island life. Babies are baptized in the church. Adults gather here for worship and fellowship and, when the time comes, the dead are interred in the cemetery of their chosen place of worship.

Even before the churches were built, Deal Island was known for its camp meetings, where congregations would gather for days of intense worship, usually led by itinerant preachers such as the legendary Joshua Thomas, "the parson of the islands." Thomas was born in Potato Neck in Somerset County in 1776, preached in many locations along the bay, finally settling in Deal Island, where he died in 1853. His grave is in the cemetery of the Methodist church on the island.

The religious nature of Deal Island brought about a change in the name of the island many years ago. According to early maps, the original name was Devil's Island, which in the local brogue was pronounced "deal's." In the early 1800s, a local church official urged that the spelling be changed to Deal's Island to eliminate any association with Satan. More recently, the possessive form of the name has been dropped, and on the official Maryland state map it simply is "Deal Island."

A brochure on Deal Island, published by the county tourism office, begins with this simple but true observation: "When you crossed the bridge, you entered a different way of life." On Deal Island, life is all about the waters of the Chesapeake Bay and its tributaries. Deal Island is at the very tip of a peninsula, or neck, that juts out into Tangier Sound. Manokin River makes up the southern boundary, Monie Bay and the Nanticoke River are to the north, and the open waters of the bay are due west. It comes as no surprise that the history and culture of this island are shaped and defined by the Chesapeake. It is the provider of jobs, the source of recreation, and for most of the people who live here, it is the fountain of their faith and inspiration.

25

Furnace Town

One of Worcester County's Hot Attractions

On one of the hotter and more humid days of July, my wife suggested that we take a little weekend trip to Furnace Town. "It's ninety in the shade," I said. "You want to go tour a furnace?"

Once we made a visit, though, and once I learned to deal with that somewhat peculiar name, I learned to enjoy Furnace Town. Now, it has become a regular destination for weekend hikes and family picnics. The place is really pretty cool.

The furnace at Furnace Town is not used to heat the place. In the 1830s, iron was made here, and the purpose of the furnace was to heat bog iron to the point where the molten iron separated from the ore. The furnace was last fired in 1850.

Nassawango Creek runs through Furnace Town, and if you look closely along the sandy, shallow bars, you often will see veins of orange or red. These stains look like some sort of odd pollution or an algae bloom, but they actually are bog iron sediments. When prospectors found these in the late 1700s, there soon began an effort to extract them and convert them to valuable iron ore.

Today, Furnace Town is a re-creation of what the village here might have been like in the 1830s. The old furnace has been stabilized, and it has been joined by many buildings that help interpret the history of iron-making along the Nassawango. Furnace Town is in the midst of The Nature Conservancy's Nassawango Creek Preserve, a sanctuary of more than 10,000 acres of forested wetland, so not only do we have a re-constructed village that accurately captures an important page of local history, but we also have an extraordinary natural area that is perfect for hiking, canoeing, picnicking, and nature study.

Furnace Town is between Snow Hill and Salisbury, about a mile west of Route 12. Traveling north from Snow Hill, turn left onto Old Furnace Road—the village will be on the left. A parking area and visitor center are at the entrance.

Kathy Fisher is the executive director of the Furnace Town Foundation, a non-profit organization established to re-create the old village and interpret its role in local history. I walked the grounds with her on one balmy spring day, enjoying the shade of the giant oaks and pines, as she explained that in the 1830s the grounds here would have been barren. Charcoal was needed to fire the giant furnace, and the forests here were cut to provide wood for that purpose. The landscape would not have been the same.

Fisher and I walked the village paths to the church, the blacksmith's shop, the broom-maker's cottage, and the weaving house. Down the hill, on the edge of the swamp, was the furnace, and beyond that a forest of thick cypress and sweet gum. I had difficulty looking at this landscape and envisioning open spaces, homes, businesses, gardens, and offices, all permanently clouded by the acrid haze of smoldering charcoal.

The town itself, while it made a dramatic change in the landscape, existed for a comparatively short while. Fisher told me the bog ore was discovered in 1788 by Joseph Widener, a prospector from Philadelphia, but efforts to extract the iron were not made until the Maryland Iron Company was formed and the state legislature offered tax incentives for the company to process the bog ore.

Initially, the company intended to remove the bog iron and transport it to a furnace in New Jersey for processing, but the Nassawango site offered advantages that made construction of a furnace here a sound business decision. Nassawango Creek flowed through the swamp and, if a canal were dug, the iron could be shipped by boat to the Pocomoke River a few miles downstream and then from there to the Chesapeake Bay and to factories all over the East Coast.

The proximity of the site to the Bay also meant an abundant supply of oyster shells, a source of calcium used in the smelting process to remove impurities from the iron ore. Perhaps most important, though, were the thousands of acres of mature trees that covered the site. Charcoal could be made, and it could be used in the furnace to heat the ore until it became molten metal, so between 1830 and 1832 the furnace was built and a town of three hundred people quickly grew around it.

"Many of the people came from New Jersey," she said. "The area here was very much like the Pine Barrens, with very sandy soil. A furnace closed there around the same time this one was built, so they moved many of the skilled people down here. The Maryland Iron Company consisted of investors from Maryland, Pennsylvania, Maine, and New Jersey, and they had interests in several iron furnaces in the region. It was a little like how business works today: a factory shuts down and the employees are given the option of moving to a new factory in another location."

While some historical villages tend to romanticize the life they re-create, Fisher does not do so with Furnace Town. "Living here had to have been a grueling experience, especially for the laborers," she said. "There were no federal agencies to ensure worker safety. There was no health insurance, no retirement plan, the pay was miserly, and the working conditions had to have been awful. Sulfur is released in the smelting process, and the odor of it permeated the town. There were always smoldering fires where the charcoal was being made, so it was smoky and hot here. The furnace didn't operate during the winter months, so it was a hot weather industry, made even hotter by the furnace and the constantly smoldering piles of timber. There was little shade, and the landscape was described at the time as a barren sand hill. Life here wasn't like something from a movie set."

Charcoal was crucial to the smelting process at Furnace Town. Charcoal makers, called colliers, would stack wood in a pile, cover the pile with dirt, and then apply low, steady heat using as little air as possible. If too much oxygen reached the wood, it would flame and burn and be reduced to ashes instead of charcoal.

"The men would go into the forest, mark out a thirty-five-foot diameter circle, and begin cutting trees and building the charcoal mound," Fisher said. "They cut everything. They were totally indiscriminate. They needed such a large volume of wood they couldn't afford to be choosy. Whatever was needed to complete the pile in the circle was cut."

Some of the wood, probably cypress, was used in the construction of businesses, homes, stores, and other buildings, but most of the forest that covered the 4,800 acres went to feed the furnace. A stream was dammed just north of the furnace, creating a pond of about three hundred acres. Mill races were built leading from the pond: one to power a gristmill where grains were processed; one to power a sawmill where timber was converted to lumber; and a third to power the bellows that superheated the charcoal in the furnace.

The furnace apparently flourished for a few years after it opened. Lewis Walker was brought in from the Speedwell Furnace in New Jersey, and he served as ironmaster, living in the large frame home in the village called the Ironmaster's Mansion. In 1832, sixty people were employed to run the furnace, with others operating satellite businesses in the town, but by the mid-1830s much of the timber surrounding the furnace had been cut, making the production of charcoal more difficult and expensive.

In 1837, the furnace ended up in the hands of Thomas Spence, who briefly gave it a new life. Spence carefully studied the technology of iron furnaces and retrofitted the old furnace with a heat exchanger imported from England. This "hot blast" system raised the temperature inside the furnace by passing the blast air through a stove heated by hot waste gases as they left the furnace. This accelerated the combustion process and decreased the amount of charcoal needed, greatly increasing the efficiency and production of the furnace. It was one of the first hot blast furnaces used in the United States.

As a result, for a time, Furnace Town again prospered. Spence turned the old ironmaster's mansion into a boarding house and he built a new, fourteen-room mansion for his family. A post office was in operation, as well as a bank and a shoemaker's shop. Spence owned a general merchandise store in nearby Snow Hill, and he ran a second business in Furnace Town, supplying residents with a wide variety of goods, from bricks for construction projects to cloth for making clothing.

The business succeeded for about a decade, but by 1850 Spence was forced to sell the furnace and the surrounding property. Development of the American railroad and canal systems gave competitors an advantage in marketing their product, making the furnace in Nassawango Swamp unprofitable.

Spence declared bankruptcy and the furnace was never again fired. Businesses shut down, most of the residents moved out, and over the years Furnace Town became a ghost town, a relic sometimes enjoyed by curious picnickers and scavenger hunters on weekends. Slowly, the old forest that surrounded the furnace became a new-growth forest. The abandoned shops and homes gave way to time, and by 1900 all that was left were a few foundations, the old slag pile, and the huge old brick furnace that seemed curiously out of place in what by then had become a mature forest.

26

On the Nassawango

This Quiet Stream May be the Best Place to Paddle on Delmarva

If I had to pick a single favorite place to paddle a canoe or kayak on the Delmarva, it would be Nassawango Creek — specifically the portion between the bridge at Red House Road and the town of Snow Hill. If you head north from Snow Hill on Route 12, turning left on Red House Road a few miles out of town, you'll soon come to a small wooden bridge that crosses a modest stream. This would be Nassawango Creek. While it doesn't look like much from the view on the bridge, launch a canoe here, head downstream into the folds of cypress, and you'll soon be in one of Delmarva's special places.

Several factors make this stretch of Nassawango special. It's narrow, winding, shallow, and filled with cypress knees and deadfalls. Motor boats don't do much business here, so for several miles the only sounds you'll hear will be sounds of the swamp: the cackle of pileated woodpeckers, the squeal of flushing wood ducks, and the booming "who-cooks-for-you" chant of barred owls.

This section of the swamp is protected, so it will remain wild for generations to come. The Nature Conservancy began a preserve here in 1978, slowly building the protected area to more than 3,000 acres, and then, in 2004, the conservancy bought 3,520 acres from the E.S. Adkins Company, more than doubling the size of the sanctuary. Since then, they've added more parcels, enlarging the preserve to more than 10,000 acres, thus making it the largest private nature preserve in Maryland.

The Nassawango is a southern cypress swamp, more comparable to habitat found in the southeastern United States than on Delmarva, where lowlands tend to be covered with grasses and flooded with saltwater. The Nassawango is fresh, even though its waters are pushed and pulled by the tidal flow of the Chesapeake Bay many miles away.

The water is glossy and black, flowing almost imperceptibly. A few hundred feet from the put-in on Red House Road, the creek takes a left turn and disappears into a fold of cypress and gum. Cypress knees grow out of the shallows on the edge of the creek; huge gums and oaks lean over the water, in summer creating a green canopy that only now and then lets the sun through.

When we're first on the creek, we tend to paddle rather hurriedly for a few minutes, but after putting some distance between us and the bridge, we stop paddling and just listen to the swamp. If we go in early spring, the number of birds we hear is amazing, even if we can identify only a few of the songs. In May, at the peak of the migration, the swamp becomes a great migratory corridor, with thousands of songbirds traveling to nesting grounds in the north. According to the conservancy, Nassawango is home to twenty-one species of warblers during migration and the nesting season.

The prothonotary warbler, a bright yellow bird sometimes called the "swamp canary," is the signature bird of the swamp. You're not likely to find prothonotaries in upland forests, as it truly is a bird that has adapted totally to swamps. It nests near the water, and sometimes will actually build in a stump, dead branch, or cypress knee over the water. By building over the water, the prothonotary escapes many of its predators, and although flooding is a possibility, prothonotary fledglings have developed the unique ability among songbirds to swim.

In addition to birds, the Nassawango is home to numerous rare plants, including twelve species of orchids. The bald cypress is the most impressive tree in the swamp, and even though most of them were cut in the early 1800s to feed the great iron furnace nearby, there are still a few huge examples, and these make a canoe trip through the swamp especially rewarding. Even though civilization is not far away, the black water, the huge trees, and the great green canopy create the illusion of wilderness, if only for a few hours.

Too many of us perceive swamps as dark, forbidding places filled with venomous snakes, clouds of biting insects, and various other dangers. The Nassawango, however, in most seasons is filled with color and is not in the least forbidding. In the spring, wild azaleas bloom along the shore, fringetree blossoms hang in white clusters, and birds, butterflies, and dragonflies skitter through the forest canopy like little jewels.

About halfway to Snow Hill is the Fran Uhler Nature Trail, a good spot to stretch the legs, have lunch, and look for wildflowers. The short trail loops from the creek shore to an upland forest, and then back through a hardwood swamp to the trail head. A second trail, called the Prothonotary Trail, was under construction at this writing. This one-mile spur off the Uhler Trail will run south along the edge of the bottomland, making a trip on the Nassawango a complete canoeing and hiking experience.

Beyond the Uhler trail take-out, the creek widens and changes character somewhat. The green canopy is replaced by open sky, and the little creek looks more like a proper river, complete with boat traffic.

From here, you can either paddle on to Snow Hill or head back to Red House Road. We enjoy the wilder and more secluded sections of the stream, so we usually stop at the nature trail site for lunch and then return to Red House Road, thus making the trip an out-and-back experience, paddling slowly among the cypress and scanning the shoreline with the binoculars for birds. It would be easy to paddle on to Snow Hill and take-out at Pocomoke River Canoe Company and catch a ride back to the car, but having explored the upper creek for a few hours, we're usually reluctant to give up this feeling of wildness, of being in a remote and special place. After all, such experiences are all too rare these days.

27

The Upper Pocomoke

Put-in at Porter's and See the Wild Pocomoke

"See any snakes?" the woman asked. She was loading her gear into a red Old Town® canoe and seemed remotely disappointed when we answered in the negative. My son, Tom, and I eased our canoes into the shallows, exited, and pulled them onto high ground. "No snakes, but lots of birds," I said.

We were on the upper part of the Pocomoke River, where it runs narrow and flat and is the color of coffee. The Porter's Crossing bridge spans the river here, and it's a good place to put-in and take-out. From the bridge, you can see about one hundred feet of river, and then it disappears into a fold of green. Huge cypress trees line the banks of the Pocomoke, their limbs creating a canopy of foliage that makes the river seem dark and mysterious.

This quality of mystery, this darkness, gives the Pocomoke a sinister quality, especially when you stand on a bridge and watch the river disappear into a cypress swamp so huge it could be endless. Our culture has taught us to be wary of swamps. In literature and films, swamps are dark places where evil lurks, but, when you enter the Pocomoke by canoe and leave the bridge behind, you will find no evil... only a place of quiet beauty where rare plants grow and colorful warblers sing in the treetops.

The Pocomoke River begins north of the Maryland and Delaware line, where it drains a huge swamp and thousands of acres of farm fields, which a few centuries ago would have been swamps as well. It winds its way southward down the peninsula, a thin blue line on the map, and doesn't widen appreciably until it nears the town of Snow Hill. From Snow Hill, it flows through forest and farmland to Pocomoke City and empties into Pocomoke Sound, which forms the boundary between Maryland and Virginia on the Eastern Shore.

The lower portions of the Pocomoke have seen very little development, but they can be busy, especially on summer weekends as fishermen and recreational boaters take to the water. If you paddle a canoe or kayak, though, the upper portions of the river can provide a timeless escape from civilization, at least for a day. Much of the woodland along the upper river is protected as state forest or through ownership by The Nature Conservancy, a private land conservation organization.

The town of Snow Hill is a good focal point for exploring the Pocomoke. The community was founded in 1642 and is named for a district in London. The river runs through the town and, in years past, was key to the commerce of the area, serving as a means of sending valuable timber and iron ore to markets. Today, the river is more often a source of recreation. A park and boat launch facility are on the river in town, and a few miles south is Pocomoke River State Park at Shad Landing. The park has campgrounds set under tall pines and hardwood trees, rental cabins, a fishing pond, boat rentals, a hiking trail, and various other amenities.

Pocomoke River Canoe Co. is located in an old lumber warehouse on Route 12 in Snow Hill, and proprietor Barry Laws offers canoe sales, rentals, and a shuttle service to convenient put-ins.

If you bring your own boat, you can put-in at various locations along the river and paddle either to Snow Hill and get a ride back to your vehicle, or simply paddle out and back. The best put-ins are where bridges cross the river along secondary roadways. Whiton Crossing is about twelve miles north of Snow Hill and Porter's is about halfway between Whiton and the town. The river here is narrow and winding, although portions between Whiton and Porter's were channelized years ago to improve storm drainage.

A third alternative would be to put-in on Nassawango Creek at the bridge on Red House Road. The Nassawango is a tributary of the Pocomoke and joins the river just south of Snow Hill. It's a six-mile paddle from Red House Road to either Snow Hill or Shad Landing.

Canoeing any of these sections of the river will provide a close-up look at a classic cypress swamp. The river is narrow and shallow, and numerous deadfalls make travel by larger boat impractical, so you can paddle all day without encountering motor boats. On weekdays, it's rare even to meet other canoeists.

It is best to approach the Pocomoke slowly, stopping frequently to float with the gentle current and enjoy the sights and sounds of the river. When we went recently, the prothonotary warblers were in the middle of nesting season, and these bright yellow and gray birds were like jewels in the treetops, especially when one was caught in a shaft of sunlight. We watched one warbler hopscotch along lillypads, chasing a damselfly. The bird was so busy tracking the insect it ignored us, nearly flying into our canoe.

The river here is flat, but there usually is a current. The water is dark and glossy, metallic almost, and the only time you realize it's moving is when you notice a leaf float by or see lillypads slow-dancing in the current. The water is fresh this far up the Pocomoke, but it still is pushed and pulled by the tides as the Chesapeake Bay ebbs and floods.

There are snakes here, but most are harmless water snakes, which, given the alternative, would prefer to have nothing to do with humans. Many people, however, see a snake on the water and assume it is a poisonous cottonmouth moccasin and dispatch it accordingly. Cottonmouths are common farther south, in the Back Bay and Dismal Swamp areas of Tidewater Virginia, but they are very rare this far north, so if you see a snake, it very likely will be a harmless species of water snake. There's an easy way to tell the difference between cottonmouths and water snakes: when swimming, cottonmouths float high on the water, like a tire tube, while water snakes are mostly submerged, with only its head above the surface.

No matter how a snake swims, though, it's always good to remember that this is its home. It belongs here and is part of the natural landscape. You're here for a few hours in your canoe. The snake, we could say, is your host, so why not treat it with the respect it deserves?

28

Shad Landing

Camping Along the Pocomoke Comes with a Few Surprises

I didn't mind the monkeys howling until they started throwing rocks — and then I was ready to get serious. I woke Lynn up. "The monkeys are attacking," I said. "They're throwing rocks."

She mumbled something, turned over in her sleeping bag, and made a drowsy declaration to the effect that the only monkey in these woods was in the sleeping bag next to hers. And then I remembered. They really are not monkeys; they just sound like it, and they're not throwing rocks. Acorns are falling from the oak trees and hitting the roof of our camper.

We had been hearing pileated woodpeckers back in the woods all evening and were making jokes about how their calls resemble the monkey soundtracks in the old "Tarzan" movies. As I dozed off, we came under monkey attack.

We were camping in Pocomoke River State Park at Shad Landing, near Snow Hill. This is one of our favorite places to camp. It's not fancy, but the campsites are spacious and nearly all are shaded by huge pines and hardwoods. A trail winds through a cypress swamp and is always a nice place to explore. There is a swimming pool available during the warmer months, a nature center, fishing pond, and numerous hikes and programs led by naturalists. There is also, of course, the river...roll on mighty Pocomoke. A boat ramp is just next to the camp store, and there are canoes and kayaks to rent if you don't feel like bringing your own. You can cast a few lures just minutes from your campsite.

I will admit up-front that we are not sophisticated campers. We have a tent and a screen house, and if we want to go upscale, we bring the old F-150 and sleep in the back. It has a fiberglass cap, and I picked up a 4' x 8' sheet of blue insulating foam at the local building supply store. This goes in the bed, followed by a cushion, and then the sleeping bags. It's a very comfortable arrangement — until you have to get up at 3 a.m. and slide down a cold and damp tailgate to go outside to pee or the monkeys start throwing rocks.

With the F-150, however, I can tow the little skiff to the park, launch the boat, and have the truck for the weekend as both a home on wheels and a means of transportation, in case the need arises to ride into Snow Hill and do some shopping. We usually forget staples such as Half & Half for the morning coffee or a Peppermint Pattie for the evening dessert.

Pocomoke River State Forest and Park is a large chunk of Eastern Shore real estate — more than 15,000 acres — so there is a lot of territory to explore. You can camp year-round at Shad Landing. Milburn Landing, down the river and on the opposite shore, offers camping from May until mid-December. Shad is by far the largest campground, with 192 sites to thirty-two at Milburn.

When we visit Shad Landing, canoeing and fishing are usually high on the agenda, but Lynn and I are both birders, so we do a lot of hiking in the spring and fall, when the migrant songbirds are passing through. Our favorite trail is called "The Trail of Change," which begins next to the Acorn Trail camping loop, where we usually try to get a site. When our son, Tom, was small, we'd hike the Trail of Change and warn him, in dire, quavering tones borrowed from an old horror movie, "Once you've entered the Trail of Change, you'll never be the same again."

Tom never quite seemed to be intimidated by that warning, realizing that it was not the hiker who was undergoing change, but the trail itself, which it does. It begins in an upland forest, winds through what long-ago was a farm site, and then continues on to a bottomland hardwood swamp, where the trail winds through cypress knees and standing water, and then through a thicket back to high land. It's a circuit hike of a mile or so, and a good reminder of how changes of just a few feet in elevation bring about great adaptations in plants and the natural communities they support. It's also a good place for birding, providing a wide range of habitat over a fairly short distance.

What we like best about Shad Landing, though, is that at the end of the day you can stoke up a good wood fire, get your clothes all smelly, put a thick hunk of red meat on the grill, and spend the evening communing with nature. We bake the potatoes at home before leaving just to be sure they're done. We also bring a bottle of Merlot to add a little sophistication to the backwoods experience.

There can be no better way to end a day outdoors: a hunk-a-hunk-a-burning protein, a buttered carb the size of your fist, and sufficient red wine to induce a monkey-filled slumber.

29

Camping at
Assateague National Seashore

Sleeping by the Surf

After a day of hiking, it's always a pleasure to fall asleep to the rumble of crashing surf. It's a wonderful, rhythmic sound, a symphony played on the bass chords, hiss and boom, advance and retreat.

Unfortunately, there are too few places where you can lie down for the night up-close and intimate with the ocean. You could rent a room at the Oceanfront and leave the patio door open, but you might end up sharing your room with a gull, or worse.

Considering the many miles of Atlantic shoreline along our coast, there are precious few places where you can unroll your sleeping bag and doze off to the sound of tumbling surf. Camping is allowed at False Cape State Park in Virginia Beach, but the camping areas are quite a distance from the ocean. Most of the remote islands on the Eastern Shore are owned by The Nature Conservancy, and while it welcomes day use, overnight camping is not allowed.

Where, then, is a weary camper to go when she longs to drift off to the ebb and flood of the ocean's rhythm? The answer is Assateague Island, where you can pitch your tent so close to the ocean you can skim a clamshell off the breaking surf with one foot still in your sleeping bag.

Most residents of southern Delmarva know Assateague as the island on the Eastern Shore where Chincoteague National Wildlife Refuge is located, herds of wild ponies roam, and tens of thousands of tourists flock in the summer to the ocean beach. It's a wonderful place, but it's not the Assateague I have in mind. They close the gates there at dark, and camping is not allowed.

Go north, young woman. Assateague is a large island, more than thirty miles long, and only part of it is in Virginia. The northern (Maryland) end of Assateague is a national seashore and state park, and here you can hike up the beach, pitch your tent, and have a refreshing sleep accompanied by surf music.

While the Virginia portion of Assateague is accessed via the town of Chincoteague, to reach the Maryland end you take Route 113 to the town of Berlin, turn right on Route 376, right again on Route 611, and make your way across Verrazano Bridge to the island.

Assateague here is low and narrow, with a few loblolly pine forests among the bayberry thickets and tidal marshes. The vulnerability of the island to storms is apparent from atop the bridge. It is a slender finger of sand, a tenuous bit of land separating Sinepuxent Bay from the Atlantic. Look north and there's the skyline of Ocean City, an unlikely oasis that hovers over the ocean.

Assateague State Park is on the Maryland end of the island, where swimming, surf fishing, and camping are allowed. The national seashore surrounds the state park and portions of that are open to camping as well.

If you bring your bicycles to Assateague, park at the visitor center just west of the bridge and take the bike path southward down the island. A pedestrian/bike bridge runs parallel to the vehicular span and then turns south with Bayberry Drive for about four miles, where it ends at a cul-de-sac. It's a great place for a bike ride, with wild ponies frequently seen along the road and little sika deer foraging in the bayberry thickets.

To enter the national seashore, stop at the entrance gate, pay the fee, and continue southward. Assateague National Seashore has three interpretive hiking trails (pedestrians only) that make interesting side trips: Life of the Marsh Trail, Life of the Forest Trail, and Life of the Dunes Trail.

Turn right on Bayside Drive just past the entrance and the "Life of the Marsh Trail" will be on the left. It's a loop of about a half-mile and offers a good view of Sinepuxent Bay and the salt marsh that makes up the bayside margin of the island. Farther along Bayberry Drive is the "Life of the Forest Trail," another half-mile loop that takes you through a loblolly pine forest, thickets of greenbrier and phragmites, and then along a transition zone where upland meets salt marsh. The wooded area is a great place to see songbirds, such as warblers and thrushes, during the spring migration. The "Life of the Dunes Trail" begins and ends at the cul-de-sac at the end of Bayberry Drive. Here you can learn how dunes are sculpted by wind, water, and other forces, and you can see an extensive variety of dune plants, such as American beachgrass and beach heather.

If you have camping on your mind, you have several choices. Bayside sites are available across the road from Life of the Marsh Trail. Most are in a wooded area and include picnic tables and charcoal grills. Closer to the beach, camping areas are provided behind the primary dune line along Bayberry Drive. These are primitive sites, with few amenities. If you want to get away from the crowds, several walk-in campsites are available farther south and canoe-in sites are situated along the bayside.

Keep in mind that this is camping in the rough. When the weather warms, insects can be bothersome, and in hot weather there is little shade to provide relief. If the wind is blowing, it's nearly impossible to keep sand out of your tent and sleeping bag, and if it's really blowing, you could find that your tent has transformed itself into a kite.

Ah, but it's worth it. Hike those trails, walk that beach, enjoy that gourmet dinner of sand-infused macaroni and cheese, and then turn in for the night. Hear that? It's the rhythm of the surf. It's wild and ancient and it reminds us how huge this world is and how small, vulnerable, and fragile we are. Now, that's something to sleep on.

30

Chicken Necking at Assateague

We Hunt, We Gather

There is something elemental about gathering your own dinner. On Delmarva, hunting and fishing are noteworthy traditions. There is nothing quite like having fresh rockfish baked with potatoes and onions, sweetened with a dollop of butter and cream. A winter dinner might consist of venison tenderloin sauted with tart apples and black walnuts in a red wine reduction or black duck slow-cooked in an orange sauce, served with Hayman potatoes and turnip greens spiked with apple cider vinegar.

These are Delmarva dining traditions based on our kinship with the countless forests, creeks, bays, streams, and guts that define our peninsula. The land and the water have fed us well.

Another aspect of hunting and gathering is even more elemental, and this would be chicken necking. Fishing usually requires a boat and a good deal of tackle. Hunting is a fine sport, but one needs guns and ammo, licenses, and other gear, not to mention a place to hunt and the time to devote to planning and preparation. You can seldom just head out the door and come back an hour later with dinner.

Not so chicken necking. Chicken necking is the time-honored Delmarva pastime of recreational crabbing. Not surprisingly, a raw chicken neck is used as bait, and when the crab takes a bite, it is brought up from the bottom, scooped up in a net, and placed in a pail. When crabs sufficient for dinner fill the pail, you take them home and steam them, pick out the flaky white meat, and enjoy one of the best dining experiences Delmarva has to offer.

There are two aspects of chicken necking that I especially enjoy. First, it is a primal sport, one virtually unchanged since the Nanticokes stalked these same creeks and guts, armed with no more than a piece of bait and a net. You can't get much more basic than that. Second, the meat of the Chesapeake Bay blue crab is probably the finest that a crustacean has to offer. Steam the crabs, pluck that meat free of the shell, dip it in a bit of butter seasoned with Old Bay, and you're in for a memorable dining experience. The wonderful thing about blue crabs is that the less you fuss over them, the better they taste. Professional chefs go through all sorts of gyrations to make gourmet crab dishes, but with Delmarva blue crabs, less is more: cook the crab and eat the meat. Not exactly complicated, is it?

On Delmarva, there are countless places to go chicken necking. Find a rural two-lane bridge that crosses a little tidal gut, and on a summer weekend there will likely be a half-dozen chicken-neckers hunched over the railing, one holding a string and another a net.

If you're worried about trespassing on private property, do your chicken necking at a public place, such as Assateague National Seashore on the Maryland end of Assateague Island. The Park Service folks actually encourage such activity and have built a boardwalk along a bayside marsh to make crabbing easy. Signs point out the crabbing area, provide helpful tips, and spell out the minimal regulations, e.g. the minimum size for jimmie (male) crabs is five inches from point to point on the shell.

Chicken necking is a great sport for children, a tasty way to indoctrinate young people in the art of hunting and gathering. Go to Assateague on a summer day, and the boardwalk will be lined with kids of all ages, some holding chicken necks on a string, their partners armed with a net to scoop up the unsuspecting crab. Teamwork is held in high regard here.

Many local families keep a supply of chicken necks in the freezer just for the purpose of catching crabs. If we're having fried chicken, the breasts and the legs go into the pan while the neck goes into the freezer bag. When it's time to go crabbing, the necks are thawed, a stout length of string is tied tightly around one, and it is dangled from a bridge or boardwalk into the water. When a crab decides to take a taste, it is usually wise to let it settle down to feed and then, when it is fully immersed in its meal, slowly lift the crab to the surface where your partner can net it. If you're on your own, it takes only a little practice to get the hang of lifting with one hand and netting with the other.

Once young people get the hang of catching crabs, it is easy to extend that interest to the life-cycle of crabs and the role they play in the bays, creeks, and salt marshes of the coast. For example, begin by determining whether a crab is male or female. The easiest way to do this is to look at the "apron" on the underside of the crab. The apron on the male is in the shape of an inverted "T." A young female will have a triangular apron, and a mature female's apron will be rounded, like a shield. A female crab ready to spawn will have a mass of orange eggs under the apron, and is called a sponge crab.

A single female crab will release millions of eggs each season, but few of these will survive to become adult crabs. Most will be eaten by various predators in the egg stage or as larval crabs. They nourish fish, such as striped bass, croaker, eels, spot, and catfish. Crabs that survive to adulthood are omnivorous eaters, feasting on small fish, shellfish, worms, crustaceans, and even dead animals and plants.

Crabs are perhaps the signature hunter-gatherers of the estuary, at once predators and vultures. They are quick, ruthless hunters that will attack most anything that moves,

and they are accomplished scavengers, with a ready appetite for dead animal and plant matter. For the hunter-gatherers among us who search the salt marshes and tidal waters for our dinner, we cannot help but admire them. They are an important part of our landscape, our culture, and our economy. They also are very tasty.

31

Berlin

Delmarva's Christmas Town Gets in the Spirit

I pulled into Berlin on an early morning during the first week of December, and, appropriately, the weatherman had given us a Christmas gift. Snow had fallen overnight, blanketing the farm fields out on Route 113, and dusting the sidewalks and parking lots downtown. Snow-melt dripped off the awnings and collected along the curbs, re-freezing in black puddles on the cold asphalt. It made walking a bit dicey, but no one seemed to mind, because Berlin was in the mood to celebrate Christmas and a little crusty snow just added to the ambiance.

Most of the towns on the Delmarva Peninsula celebrate Christmas, even if it means just a few strings of lights along Main Street. Some have parades, others have concerts, and a few have banquets and caroling. Berlin has all of this — and much more. Christmas starts early here and is celebrated on a daily basis.

Berlin is a beautiful town, filled with historic homes and businesses, and it has a lively downtown, with interesting shops, antique markets, and restaurants. Unlike many small towns that have fallen victim to the big box retailers that set up shop in the suburbs, Berlin's downtown seems to be thriving, thanks to creative retailers who have carved their own marketing niche and know how to capitalize on the history and charm of an old downtown that literally has been a movie set. (Portions of *Runaway Bride* and *Tuck Everlasting* were filmed in Berlin.)

Berlin's fascination with celebrating Christmas began as a marketing tool — a way to encourage folks to shop downtown instead of at the shopping center — but it has evolved to become much more than that. The celebration begins around the time of Thanksgiving with a tree-lighting ceremony at the old Atlantic Hotel and goes on for a month, with carriage rides, art shows, model train displays, bell choirs, concerts, home tours, dinners, high teas, breakfasts with Santa, and, of course, the Christmas parade. As a result, Berlin attracts December visitors not only from across Delmarva, but from all over the Mid-Alantic.

"It began in the early 1990s," said Debbie Frene, one of the current organizers. "A few of the downtown merchants decided to have a Victorian Christmas, so they dressed up in costume and got a horse and carriage to give people rides through the old part of town, but it was just for one weekend during Christmas. Eventually, more people joined in and the celebration grew. We added 'Breakfast with Santa,' and people really loved the carriage rides, so we decided to have them each Friday and Sunday during December. We found someone with a huge collection of animated Christmas figures, so a number of the merchants purchased these and are using them as window displays, and local businesses, organizations, and churches are now adding their own programs as part of the celebration."

For example, the downtown Tea by the Sea shop hosts a Holiday High Tea with a Christmas theme, as well as Tea with Mrs. Claus. The Solstice Restaurant celebrates the winter solstice with an appropriate feast on December 21st. A progressive holiday dinner includes a five-course meal at four downtown restaurants, and the Buckingham Presbyterian Church hosts a breakfast buffet with Santa as the special guest.

In addition, there is a special evening set aside for local artists to display their works. Shops remain open late on Friday evenings, and there are many occasions to enjoy Christmas music and carols. "It began with just a few merchants," said Frene, "but it has become a real Berlin thing. The entire community is involved."

As a result, Berlin attracts visitors from as far away as Philadelphia and New York, who come for an old time, small town celebration of Christmas. You could call it an Irving Berlin production come to life. "We're in a unique situation here," says Frene. "Many people have summer homes, second homes, not far from Berlin, so they come and spend a weekend here. I do mailings to Philadelphia, Baltimore, New York, New Jersey, and people come. We get local folks from around Delmarva and people from off Delmarva who want to come to Berlin to shop. Shopping here is not like going to the mall. We have things they can't find there, and the atmosphere is totally different. All the shop owners run their own businesses — we don't just work nine to five — and we care about what people buy. Christmas shopping can be stressful. Here, we make it relaxing. That's what Christmas should be."

32

Ocean City
in the Off-season

Winter Is a Great Time to Go to the Beach

From the ninth floor of an oceanfront hotel in Ocean City, the view is panoramic. The ocean is laid out like a huge sheet of shimmering steel, and the sun sparkles as the waves break far below. About a mile offshore a trawler chases a school of fish, its booms outstretched like the wings of a giant insect. Gulls follow in its wake, hoping to dine on discards. Just beyond the breakers, surf scoters trade back and forth; with the binoculars, I can make out the bright orange bill and the white nape.

It is an intensely beautiful scene, ever-changing, and it is the dead of winter, the perfect time to go to the beach. Lynn and I checked in late in the afternoon, unpacked, and relaxed on the balcony with the binoculars. The temperature was nudging fifty, and in the shelter of the walled balcony it was not at all uncomfortable. On the beach below, a solitary figure was walking her dog; otherwise, the place was ours, or so it seemed.

Gradually, the sky darkened, turning purple just before night fell, and soon a full moon rose, emerging from the ocean like molten metal, becoming hard and fast as it cleared the horizon. We could see the craters and gullies through the binoculars. The show was so spectacular we decided to forego dinner in the restaurant and instead ordered a pizza, having dinner on the ninth floor as we watched one of nature's great dramas.

The denouement came a little before 7 p.m., when the top right corner of the full moon suddenly disappeared, as if something had taken a bite. In minutes, the shadow broadened, and soon all that was left of the moon was a bright, brief outline, the majority darkened by the shadow of the Earth, which for a few precious moments was positioned between the moon and sun, creating a lunar eclipse of the first order.

Most people associate the beach with summer, as if on Labor Day someone comes along with a giant key and locks everything up until spring. In my mind, winter is the perfect time to go to the beach. True, the water is too cold for swimming, but the view from an oceanfront room is, if anything, more spectacular in winter than in summer, and many of the things we enjoy in the warmer months, such as playing golf, can be done year-round. The only things missing in the winter are the crowds and the peak season rental rates, neither of which I enjoy.

Especially appealing in the winter are the off-season bargains at the hotels. In many cases, you can book a room in a premium oceanfront hotel for less than you'd pay at a roadside motel a few miles inland and, if you go mid-week, you can really find some bargains. Even many restaurants have special offers for off-season visitors.

While mid-winter might be a little bitter for frolicking on the beach, the season does have other things to offer. Lynn and I enjoy birding and hiking, and the Ocean City area has plenty to offer in the wintertime. We watched sea ducks, gulls, and northern gannets from the comfort of our room and then we drove south to the inlet, set up the scope, and checked out the ducks and other waterfowl foraging in the current. Across the inlet is Assateague Island, and the national seashore there has several miles of hiking trails covering dunes, maritime forest, and wetlands. The birding there is excellent in the winter, and in early spring migrating songbirds will fill the maritime forest and shrub thickets.

If golfing is your idea of the perfect outdoor sport, more than a dozen courses are in the area. Some of the hotels offer packages that include oceanfront lodging, meals, golf and golf lessons, and even spa treatments. The best rates, of course, are during the winter months.

We enjoy walking the boardwalk in the wintertime, as long as the weather isn't too bitter. The south end of Ocean City, with its clapboard houses and hotels, wide porches overlooking the beach, retains the charm that made it famous among vacationers in the 1940s. The architecture is eclectic, a mix of old and new, and there is a funky mix of food and entertainment — game stands, rides, a horror house, and, of course, those famous boardwalk fries and caramel popcorn. In the summertime, the south end of the boardwalk can be noisy and crowded, with thousands of vacationers in town, but in the winter, the boardwalk is often empty, and although many of the businesses close for the season, you have a chance to study the architecture, the framework of the place, without the distraction of crowds.

A drive of fifteen minutes or so provides great opportunities for shopping and sightseeing. Head north on Route 528 and you'll parallel the oceanfront, passing through the newer part of Ocean City with its high-rises and restaurants, and in a few minutes you'll be in Fenwick Island, on the Delaware state line. Farther north, on Route 1, will be the undeveloped beaches of Fenwick Island and the Delaware Seashore State Parks and communities of South Bethany, Bethany, Dewey Beach, and Rehoboth Beach, another oceanfront resort with boardwalk, hotels, restaurants, and shops.

If it's shopping you crave, head west on Route 50 and explore the factory outlets in West Ocean City. Head even farther west and take the exit for the historic town of

Berlin, where the movies *Runaway Bride* and *Tuck Everlasting* were filmed. It's also the birthplace of naval hero Stephen Decatur. The town center has been renovated and there are numerous architectural gems in both the downtown section and in the residential area. The National Register of Historic Places lists numerous structures in Berlin, representing two centuries of architectural heritage. The town center has a large antiques mall, restaurants, shops, galleries, and historic buildings, such as the Globe Theatre and Atlantic Hotel, and winter is the perfect time to visit.

33

Pemberton Hall Plantation

History and Natural History at a Salisbury Park

This could possibly be the perfect setting for a Sunday picnic: a plantation home lovingly restored, miles of wooded hiking trails, a pond, a river, and acres and acres of open space. This would be Pemberton Hall Plantation and Pemberton Historic Park just west of Salisbury, off Route 349.

What we have here are two separate entities that blend perfectly to capture the history and natural history of this area along the Wicomico River, a few miles downstream from Salisbury. The historic brick home, built in 1741, was derelict until the Pemberton Hall Foundation was formed to restore it to its eighteenth-century appearance. The home and two surrounding acres are owned and managed by the foundation. This little island of history sits among 262 acres of protected forest and farmland known as the Pemberton Historic Park, which maintains three of the original plantation boundaries of 1750. The park is maintained by the Wicomico County Department of Parks, Recreation, and Tourism.

This is a wonderful public resource, an historic setting blended with a natural area that is remarkably diverse, ranging from brackish marshes and upland forest to open meadow. Whether you're interested in history, nature study, or are simply looking for a place for a quiet walk, Pemberton comes highly recommended.

First, a little about Pemberton Hall Plantation. Isaac Handy purchased 970 acres of land along the Wicomico River from Joseph Pemberton in 1726. Handy came to America as an indentured servant, but after paying off his indenture, he became a wealthy planter and businessman and was one of the founders of what is now the city of Salisbury. Handy established a thriving plantation, with access to the river making the site a hub of eighteenth-century commerce. He was a planter, ship owner, and was very involved in regional politics. Isaac and his wife, Anne, built the brick, gambrel-roof home in 1741 and the plantation thrived for many years. The flat, sandy soil was ideal for growing tobacco, grain, and other crops, and the streams that fed the river provided power for the mills. The large wharf along the Wicomico was a shipping point for farm goods headed to Britain and other foreign and domestic markets.

Over the years, as markets and farming practices changed, the plantation was reduced in size, the buildings fell into disrepair, and the old plantation house was in danger of destruction. Fortunately, the building has been restored, and it has been furnished with items based on eighteenth century probate inventories taken on the plantation. What visitors see today is an outstanding example of Eastern Shore regional architecture, which, together with period items, reflect what daily life might have like more than 250 years ago.

Pemberton Hall is in a park-like setting, which has become increasingly important because this area of Salisbury has experienced intense residential and commercial development in the past few years. Not long ago the park was open space amid other open spaces, but the surrounding farmland has gradually given way to homes, condominium communities, and shopping centers and office complexes. As a result, the 262 acres of farm and forest surrounding Pemberton Hall have become an oasis of green in an area that is quickly becoming developed.

Pemberton Park has seven trails, varying in distance from about one-third of a mile to a little more than a mile. If you feel like a more substantial workout, you could hike them all and rack up about five miles in total. However, the trails are intended to display the history and natural history of Pemberton, so it would be a shame to rush through them. All of the trails are well maintained and an easy walk. They are color coded, and a free brochure describes in detail the area you'll be hiking.

The History Trail, for example, is short (about a half-mile), but it crosses several sites that were important when the plantation was operating. There is a dam and a bridge to Bell Island, a site where a tannery once stood, and Mulberry Landing, now a canoe launch, but in 1746 an important docking area for ships.

Pondside Trail and Woodland Trail cover much of the same territory, with the former running close to the edge of a narrow pond created by damming a small creek. Woodland Trail winds through a mature forest, with stands of beech, white oak, and maple.

The Bell Island Trail is the longest, at 1.2 miles, and it makes accessible a widely diverse habitat. The trail begins near the main parking area, crosses a hardwood swamp, and then skirts the headwaters of a brackish creek, where lilies bloom in the summer. The trail then reaches the shoreline of the Wicomico River, runs along it for some distance, and offers great views of the river and the wildlife it supports.

Bell Island also is important in Pemberton history. In the eighteenth century, the Handy family pastured their cattle here. The area was known then as The Commons. Later, an icehouse was located on the island, and the remains of an ice pond can still be seen. This is a good place to see wildlife. Deer are plentiful, bald eagles soar overhead, and osprey arrive in March to begin nesting and fishing on the river. In the fall and winter, the open waters of the river will have numerous ducks and geese, which feed on wild rice and other grains that grow in the shallow water.

When it's time to break out that picnic lunch, you have numerous choices at Pemberton. Picnic tables are numerous near the parking area and the plantation house, a short walk from the parking area. If you really want to have a secluded spot, you can have your own picnic table on your own little island. Along the Pondside Trail is a short path that leads down to the pond, across a bridge, and to a small island that sits in the middle of the pond. It's a tiny island, with room for only one table, but if you time it right you can dine on what will be, temporarily, an island all your own.

34

The Ward Museum of Wildfowl Art

It's Not Just About Bird Carvings

On a first visit to the Ward Museum of Wildfowl Art in Salisbury, it's easy to come away with the impression that the museum is all about carved birds, whether it's antique hunting decoys or modern, highly-detailed renderings of wildfowl. After all, the museum has the most extensive collection of bird-carvings in the world.

In recent years, though, the Ward Museum has broadened its base to include more than decoys and decorative carvings. Today, it also explores the cultural context in which they were created and used. "Art, nature, and culture...that's the triad for us," said museum director Lora Bottinelli. "Art doesn't exist in a vacuum, and the museum has a responsibility to reflect the reason this genre exists, to examine why people do it, and appreciate it. Art is about nature, and both exist in a cultural setting that is unique to the people who produce it."

The Ward Museum has had a long association with Salisbury University. The original museum opened in the 1970s in a former dining hall at what was then Salisbury State College. In 1991, a new, modern facility was opened at Schumaker Pond, east of the campus. It includes six galleries, a gift shop, administrative offices and storage space, and a workshop where classes and seminars are held. The museum is operated by the non-profit Ward Foundation, but still comes under the administrative umbrella of the university.

The museum has also broadened its tie with the community in recent years. A hiking trail loops around Schumaker Pond, site of an old gristmill, and connects with the Salisbury Urban Greenway, a walking trail that winds through the city. "When people visit the museum, we want them to have a complete experience," Bottinelli explained. "The collection still provides the 'wow moment,' but after they've toured the galleries they can get out on the trail, explore the millpond, and then hike a wooded trail to the Salisbury Zoo. It's less than a half-mile away."

Museum programs have also become more diversified. Not long ago, workshops at the Ward Museum dealt strictly with bird-carving. However, recent classes have included a "Delmarva Cooks" presentation on how to cook a wild goose, which lends an entire new meaning to the term "bird carving." Other classes have demonstrated how to butcher and cook a deer and how to make homemade scrapple.

"When hunting decoys were made back in the early 1900s, the function was to lure birds to within gun range," said Bottinelli. "Hunting was a sport to wealthy people visiting coastal hunting clubs, but it was a way of life to people who lived in these communities. Wild game and fish were a regular part of most diets, so hunting and preparing food taken in the wild are part of the coastal culture. Recipes and cooking methods have been passed down in families for generations, and each coastal community has its own way of making special dishes, such as clam chowder, so art relates to nature, and it relates to culture."

Still, the driving force behind the Ward Museum is the extensive collection of bird-carvings, and it is the reason most people visit the museum in the first place. It truly is an incredible resource and, whether or not they are interested in hunting and nature, people can't help being impressed. The skill required to render what appears to be a living bird from a block of wood is astounding.

The museum has six galleries, four of which hold permanent collections and two that change presentations several times a year. One gallery features antique decoys from the various flyways of North America; another captures the life and work of the Ward brothers, Lem and Steve, who are credited with taking decoy-making to a more decorative, detailed approach. A third gallery, called "The Decoy in Time," traces the development of the hunting decoy from Native Americans to modern time, while the last gallery features contemporary carvings, many of which were winners of the annual Ward World Championship Wildfowl Carving Competition held each April at the convention center in Ocean City. Others have been donated by artists and private collectors from around the country.

At one time, the winning carvings from the April world championship became part of the museum's permanent collection. This practice has since been discontinued (winners are on display for one year and then are returned to the artist), but the museum is still responsible for many of the pieces on display. The museum traces bird-carving from its roots, when the function was to lure birds to the gun, to what today is considered decorative art intended for the human eye rather than the eye of a passing black duck.

"We like to think of the Ward Museum as more than just a place where wildfowl art is displayed," said Bottinelli. "We want to be a community center where we incorporate creativity with the environment. We have wonderful art on display, but our mission also is to show people how and why it was created."

35

The Salisbury Zoo

It's All Happening Here

There were second-graders drawing pictures, moms pushing babies in strollers, teenagers taking pictures of each other, husbands and wives relaxing together, and senior citizens sitting on park benches. The old Simon and Garfunkel song had it right: it's all happening at the zoo.

Did you notice that I didn't even mention the animals? That would mean a jaguar, a spectacled bear, capybaras, llamas, sandhill cranes, prairie dogs, bison, and colorful pink flamingos, just for starters. It was a warm summer day at the Salisbury Zoo and only the monkeys — and the humans — seemed interested in doing much. The spectacled bear swung in her hammock, the prairie dogs napped, and the flamingos stood around looking like lawn ornaments that now and then moved.

The Salisbury Zoo is Delmarva's only zoo. It's not huge when compared to its big city cousins, but it is a fine place to spend a day. The zoo is in downtown Salisbury, on a branch of the Wicomico River, and it is connected to the city park and the Ward Museum of Wildfowl Art and Schumaker Pond by an urban greenway. The zoo and the park offer solace to those who work downtown and need a quiet getaway, but it offers even more to visitors who have the time to stay awhile.

The Salisbury Zoo began in 1954 when some animals were placed on exhibition in the city park. The zoo was enlarged and improved upon in the 1970s and now has animals from North, South, and Central America in naturalistic enclosures. The mission of the zoo is to provide recreation and education, and to encourage an appreciation of wildlife and conservation of our natural world. The zoo is open everyday except Christmas and Thanksgiving. Admission is free, although donations are appreciated.

The Salisbury Zoo is not simply a park where animals and birds are displayed for public enjoyment. The zoo is an active participant in many community events, especially those dealing with conservation and natural history. A wildlife art show is held each June, and in April the zoo participates in Earth Day activities and in the Delmarva Birding Weekend. Zoo Camp is held each summer for children from kindergarten through eighth grade, providing a variety of programs dealing with conservation and environmental stewardship. For the younger set, "storytime" is held on a regular schedule in the visitor center for preschoolers (accompanied by an adult, of course). The zoo is also very active in the local school system.

In 2007, the zoo celebrated the 400th anniversary of the founding of Jamestown by building the Delmarva Trail, which features exhibits of wildlife described by Captain John Smith during his voyages in the Chesapeake Bay from 1607 to 1609. The exhibit includes whitetail deer, wild turkey, wood duck, beavers, and red wolves.

The regular exhibits include the only bear native to South America. The light coloration around the eyes give the bear its name: the spectacled bear. The Salisbury Zoo bear is a female that was born in the Baltimore Zoo in 1973. In the wild, these bears live in the cloud forests of Venezuela, Peru, Equador, Bolivia, and Columbia.

Another popular animal at the zoo is the North American bison, commonly known as the buffalo. These animals were once widespread in the western plains and prairies, but their population dwindled as the western United States was settled. The zoo has four bison, one male and three females.

One of the most beautiful animals in the zoo is the jaguar, a native of the jungles of Central and South America. These huge cats once lived in the United States, but were eradicated by hunting and trapping. The jaguar once was prized for its fur and now is a protected species.

Not surprisingly, the Salisbury Zoo has a large collection of waterfowl, and artists studying bird carving at the nearby Ward Museum often visit the zoo to gather reference material for their projects. Many of the ducks and geese are native to Delmarva while others, such as the flamingos, are not. The pair of Florida sandhill cranes are native to that state and the Okefenokee Swamp area of Georgia. They look similar to the great blue heron, which is a Delmarva native. The great blue on exhibit at the zoo was injured in the wild and is blind.

Perhaps the most popular animal at the zoo, at least among children, is the spider monkey, a native of the rainforests of Central and South America. The long limbs of these monkeys allow them to climb easily through treetops, something many eight-year-olds would like to emulate.

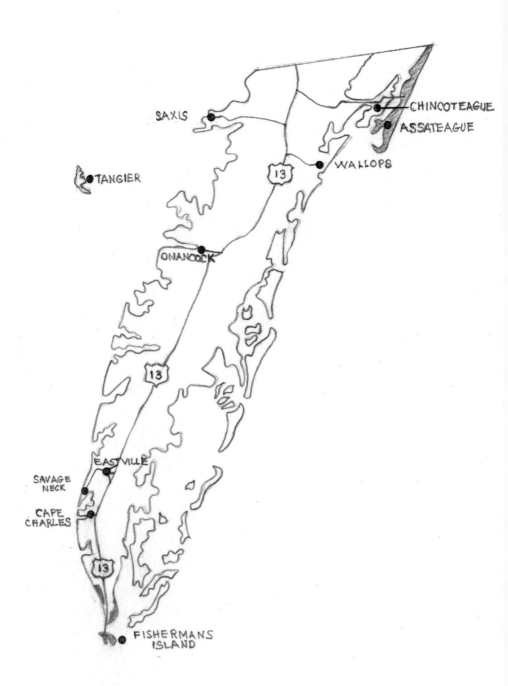

SAXIS

CHINCOTEAGUE

ASSATEAGUE

TANGIER

13 WALLOPS

ONANCOCK

13

EASTVILLE

SAVAGE
NECK

CAPE
CHARLES

13

FISHERMANS
ISLAND

VIRGINIA

Virginia Adventures

■ ■ ■

Virginia

Virginia is the last of the three Delmarva states, but by no means the least. It forms the southern portion of the peninsula, and is a narrow and mainly rural strip of land. This part of Virginia is not a major shopping destination like Dover or Salisbury. It is rich in history, although it plays its history hand with subtlety — there are no state houses, capitols, or famous battle sites. This Virginia is not known as a major tourist destination; there are no casinos, no NASCAR tracks, no oceanfront high-rises. The town of Chincoteague, with its wild pony roundup each summer and nearby beach on Assateague Island, is about the closest thing this Virginia has to what most would consider a bon-a-fide tourist draw.

Yet, many people value highly a chance to visit this friendly and somewhat remote peninsula. The lure of the Virginia portion of Delmarva is that it lacks a lot of the things other areas have created to entice visitors to the area. Let me explain this bit of convoluted logic.

Virginia's Eastern Shore does not have an Ocean City. There are no boardwalks, no oceanfront condos, no amusement parks overlooking the ocean. What it does have is 40,000 acres of coastal wilderness, a pristine landscape of barrier islands, marshes, and upland forest unmarked by roads, residences, and other amenities. People find value in that and they come to experience it. Not all of us want extensive beach-front development and the fact that Virginia lacks it is not a negative, but a plus.

The Virginia portion of Delmarva is sparsely populated; about 45,000 people live in the two counties of Accomack and Northampton. You won't find crowds here — unless you come to Chincoteague on Pony Penning Day — and many people find that a positive, not a negative.

There's not a lot of development in Virginia, at least compared to waterfront communities farther north in Maryland and Delaware. I live in Virginia, and sometimes I take this wealth of open space for granted. When working on this book, I went boating with a friend in northern Maryland. He said he wanted to show me a special place, so we rounded a bend and came upon a cove without a marina or subdivision. "It's like it was when Captain John Smith landed," he said in a reverential tone. I didn't want to be discourteous, but I was thinking, "My gosh, we have miles of landscape like this in Virginia."

There again, lacking what some communities see as a draw is not necessarily a bad thing. We don't all want marinas and subdivisions in our lives. As a result, getaways in Virginia tend to be "far from the madding crowd" experiences. We go fishing on an uninhabited barrier beach, we collect clams on a tidal flat, we go after "a nice mess of fish," and we explore remote waterways in small boats. We paddle a canoe not to reach a destination, but simply to spend some time alone with our thoughts.

These are the kinds of things Virginia offers, and you can't sum them up in a travel brochure and put it in a rack at the visitor center. Here, you'll find it rewarding to discover some things on your own, without maps and brochures to guide you.

36

Chincoteague

A Bicycle-Friendly Wildlife Refuge

Our family has for years enjoyed bicycle riding on national wildlife refuges. Most of the refuges on Delmarva allow bike riding, most provide trails specifically for biking and hiking, and at least one refuge actively encourages visitors to come by bike. This would be the Chincoteague National Wildlife Refuge on the southern (Virginia) portion of Assateague Island.

A bike trail leads from the town of Chincoteague across a bridge to Assateague, where the trail links with various wildlife-viewing circuits on the refuge. If you come by bike, you bypass the fee booth, meaning access to the refuge is free. Once on the refuge, you can ride nearly ten miles without repeating yourself. If you want to combine a bike ride with a trip to the beach, a bike trail provides direct access to the ocean.

Chincoteague's bike-friendly attitude is part of the refuge's plan to deal with visitation. The island draws a lot of visitors, especially during the summer when tens of thousands of tourists flock to the ocean/beach. Storms and a rising sea level have played havoc with parking areas, so the refuge is encouraging visitors to leave the car in town and come by bike. It makes sense. Bicycles are quiet, they don't pollute, and they take up precious little space — and for bicycle riders, the trails at Chincoteague provide a safe, pleasurable way to combine a bike ride with a little commune with nature. There are no barking dogs to contend with, no trucks coming up from behind doing sixty, no cars passing uncomfortably close.

Take the bike to Chincoteague in the fall or winter and your ride might be accompanied by a chorus of thousands of snow geese. You'll see ducks and shorebirds, herons and egrets, small Oriental elk called sika, whitetail deer, and perhaps even a famous Chincoteague pony. During the spring and fall migrations, you can park the bike along a wooded trail and see warblers, tanagers, thrushes, and other songbirds as they pause to refuel at Chincoteague before heading on. The refuge was created to provide a sanctuary for migrating waterfowl, but the forests and shrub thickets are also a vital stopover habitat for migrating songbirds as they travel between winter homes in the tropics and summer breeding grounds in the northern United States and Canada.

The best place to begin a trail ride at Chincoteague is the parking lot at the old visitor center, which is on the left a short distance past the refuge entrance. If you ride

your bike onto the refuge from town, the trail will enter the parking lot about a quarter-mile from the bridge. The parking lot is adjacent to the Wildlife Loop, a 3.2-mile paved roadway that winds around the southern impoundments on the refuge. The loop is a great place to see wildfowl during most seasons. In the fall and winter, the ponds will have snow geese, Canada geese, tundra swans, and a great variety of ducks. The loop is open to hikers and bikers, and motor vehicles are permitted from 3 p.m. until dusk.

The loop provides access to three other trails. From the parking lot, a trail runs south, parallel to Beach Road, to the Bateman visitor center and then through the woods toward the beach to provide access to Woodland Trail, a 1.6-mile paved loop through a loblolly pine forest. This is a great place to see songbirds during the spring and fall migration and the endangered Delmarva fox squirrel. It also has a panoramic viewing platform that usually offers a look at wild Chincoteague ponies.

A second trail intersecting Wildlife Loop is called Black Duck Marsh Trail, which also connects the loop with Woodland Trail. Farther along Wildlife Loop is Swan Cove Trail, which at one time ran behind the dunes, parallel to the oceanfront, to the northernmost parking lot at the beach. This trail was subject to periodic over-wash during storms, so the refuge shortened it. Swan Cove Trail now provides easy bicycle access to the beach. Turn right off Wildlife Loop and the trail comes to an end at the beach about a mile

M.A. CLARKE

north of the northernmost parking lot. The beach access point is about a half-mile from Wildlife Loop. It has a bike rack, bench, toilet, and emergency call box.

The goal of America's wildlife refuge system has always been to provide sanctuary for wildlife species, but now and then a happy corollary of that goal benefits humans, especially those of us who enjoy hiking and biking. Exposing the public to protected areas such as those at Chincoteague NWR fosters an appreciation for what the U.S. Fish and Wildlife Service is doing to create and improve these preserves. Also, by being bike-friendly, the refuge is encouraging us to leave the car at home and enjoy a unique experience with wildlife on foot or on two wheels. For those of us who are concerned about our carbon footprint, this is indeed good news.

37

Assateague Seldom Seen

Now and Then, Visitors Get to See More of the Island

There was a hawk high in a pine snag and I had the binoculars on it, but I couldn't make it out, and then it turned toward me. Once I saw those familiar mutton chops, I knew I was looking at a peregrine falcon. Peregrines are not exactly common on Delmarva, so each sighting is something to be noted.

Peregrines are magical birds to me: sleek, athletic hunters capable of great speed. Nearly wiped out in the 1960s, they are now making a comeback. It is a lion of a bird, a rare and gifted hunter, a great prize when kings and princes practiced falconry. This is a bird with royal blood.

As I watched the falcon, another bird appeared behind it, soaring in the distance, coming toward us. It was a large bird, its wings flat as it coasted on a thermal, and I realized I was looking at a peregrine falcon and a bald eagle in the same view through the binoculars. The eagle came nearer, and there was no mistaking it. A juvenile bird, perhaps in its second year, it had a dark head and belly, its wing coverts speckled with white. In two more years, it would have the characteristic white head, white tail, and yellow beak of the mature eagle. Bald eagles have been nesting in the area in recent years, so this must have been one of the fledglings.

I was on the Wildlife Loop at Chincoteague National Wildlife Refuge on Assateague Island, getting ready to head up the service road to the northern portions of Assateague, which normally are off-limits to visitors driving vehicles. It was Thanksgiving weekend, though, and the refuge was celebrating Waterfowl Week. As part of the festivities, visitors are allowed a few hours each day on the unpaved service road that runs up the spine of the island toward Maryland. I thought I'd drive up the island, scope out the northern impoundments, and see some territory I don't normally see. I suspected, however, that the trip might be anti-climactic. It would be hard to top seeing a peregrine and a bald eagle in the same binocular view.

Assateague is a large island, incorporating both Maryland and Virginia. The wildlife refuge is on the southern portion, and the island stretches northward for some thirty-seven miles across the state line and into Maryland. Jurisdiction is shared

between the U.S. Fish and Wildlife Service, which operates the refuge in Virginia, and the National Park Service, which operates Assateague National Seashore. Jurisdiction is shared along two miles of beach in Virginia. The state of Maryland has Assateague State Park on the northern part of the island.

Most visitors to Assateague see either the refuge on the Virginia end or the state park and national seashore facilities up north, but a lot of territory lies between these two outposts and a chance to explore the service road means seeing a little bit of Assateague that is off the beaten path.

The service road begins just off Wildlife Loop, the 3.2-mile paved circle that extends around freshwater impoundments on the refuge. Actually, the road is open to hikers most of the time, but few people venture all the way to the cul-de-sac that marks the effective end of the road. It's about a fourteen-mile round-trip hike. In warm weather, the legendary Assateague mosquitos and biting flies can be formidable, and in cold weather, a hike up north can be windy and uncomfortable, so we take this Thanksgiving treat for what it is — an opportunity to see some of the northern portions of this preserve in relative comfort, the heater blowing warm air and a sandwich of leftover turkey, dressing, and cranberry sauce stashed in the cooler.

The service road runs through a wooded area for the first mile or so, with pine woods on the left and a swampy thicket on the right. This is a good place to look for songbirds. In late November, yellow-rumped warblers are numerous. Now and then, wood ducks will flush from the shallow water on the right. The endangered Delmarva Peninsula Fox Squirrel is prominent in this area and, in November, can often be seen collecting pine cones and mushrooms. While Assateague is known for its waterfowl and migrating songbirds, it also has a resident population of wild turkeys, which sometimes can be seen in the pine woods.

Farther along, the landscape opens up, with freshwater impoundments on the right and shallow tidal water on the western side of the causeway. Huge flocks of snow geese are common on the refuge all winter, and these northern impoundments will often have thousands of birds, as well as black ducks, pintails, shovelers, and various other shallow water ducks.

At some places, the service road separates tidal waters and freshwater impoundments by only a short distance. These spots are great places to look for ducks, and shorebirds can usually be seen foraging along the marshy tumps on the west side of the road. Wading birds, such as the great blue herons and great egrets, are numerous, and mergansers, ruddy ducks, cormorants, and common loons can be seen in the deeper water.

In addition to the birds, a creature of the four-legged persuasion garners a great deal of attention among most visitors. This would be the famous Chincoteague pony, and herds of them can often be seen grazing along the service road. When I drove north, I found a traffic jam about a mile from the end of the road. As I guessed, a small herd of about a dozen ponies was along the roadside, their coats thick and healthy-looking with winter approaching. Cars had stopped, the cameras had come out, and visitors were documenting this very special aspect of Chincoteague wildlife.

For me, the opportunity to drive north on the service road is a chance not only to see wildlife, but also to witness this barrier island landscape in its natural setting, away from the trails, parking areas, and visitor center. On the eastern side is the breaking ocean and a string of dunes running parallel to the breakers for miles. To the west is vast salt marsh and shallow tidal bays, dotted here and there with blinds used by duck hunters. Far in the distance is the town of Chincoteague. I saw no more peregrines and bald eagles, but it was a refreshing site: Assateague as it is seldom seen.

38

NASA Wallops Island

Exploring Delmarva's Connection to Space Exploration

At the NASA Visitor Center at the Wallops Flight Facility, you can take an elevator to the roof, spread out a blanket, and lie back and take in a meteor shower, a lunar eclipse, or the launch of a rocket headed for space from nearby Wallops Island. I had buzzed by the visitor center many times, driving back and forth to Chincoteague on Route 175, unaware of this wonderful venue — and then I met Deanna Hickman, manager of the visitor center.

On a winter morning, we took the elevator up, stepped out onto the observation deck, and had a clear view some ten miles across the salt marsh to Chincoteague. Behind us, to the west, was the Wallops main base and its system of runways, the radar facilities of the NOAA weather station, the flight tower, hangars, offices, and other buildings that keep the planes flying and the rockets headed for space. To the south was Wallops Island, the remote barrier beach where rockets have been launched since the waning days of World War II, a little-known player in the early development of America's space program.

It was a surprising view. With the flat terrain of the Eastern Shore, all you need is an increase in elevation of thirty or forty feet and your perspective changes dramatically. "The main runway runs parallel to Route 175," explained Hickman, "so the observation deck gives visitors a great view when planes are taking off and landing or doing touch-and-goes. You can see much more than you can from the road."

The observation deck also comes in handy when NASA is conducting launches or when astronomical events are going on, such as eclipses and meteor showers. "The deck is open during normal operating hours, and if a special event is going on, such as the launch of a major rocket, we'll open just for that," said Hickman. "It's the best place around to view rocket launches, and it's absolutely free. There's no admission fee at all. The last time there was a major launch we had visitors here at 3 a.m."

The NASA Visitor Center is more than just a place to watch rocket launches. The Wallops Flight Facility has been a major player in space exploration for decades. Over the years, Wallops has been NASA's most active launch range, conducting more than

15,000 rocket missions since 1945. The visitor center documents the role Wallops has played in space flight, from the early sub-orbital flights and the balloon explorations of Mars, to manned flights of recent years. Wallops has managed NASA's balloon program since 1982, launching some twenty-five flights per year.

Rocketry at the Wallops Flight Facility began late in World War II, when NASA's predecessor, the National Advisory Committee for Aeronautics, chose Wallops Island as a remote test range. Engineers from the Langley Aeronautical Laboratory in Hampton used the island to perform flight research. After the war, research continued with a goal of launching a rocket that could escape the earth's atmosphere, leading to development of America's space program.

At the visitor center, you can learn all about the early role Wallops played in space research, and the changing exhibits interpret the many current programs Wallops is involved in. An important role of the visitor center, Hickman said, is education and the facility has worked hard to play a role in the curriculum of local school systems and community groups.

"We have an educator resource center here and we work with schoolteachers, scout leaders, civic groups, anyone who has an interest in Wallops and its role in space exploration," she explained. "In July and August, we supply classroom materials to teachers. We have an open house and they can come in and just pick out whatever they want. All the materials are free."

The center also plays a more active role with young people interested in rocketry and space flight. A model rocket launch is held on the first Saturday of each month, and enthusiasts can bring their own rockets and launch them at the Wallops site. In addition, programs for young people are held each weekend. "Our long history here and our unique capabilities make Wallops an ideal laboratory for the development of aerospace education," Hickman said. "We have weekly programs, hands-on exhibits, and the opportunity for young people to win a 'Space Ace' certification. All the programs encourage children to learn about technologies used by NASA researchers and scientists."

39

Saxis Wildlife Management Area
This Remote Bayside Site is a Great Place to Explore

Like Deal Island in Maryland, Virginia's Saxis Island is separated from the mainland by a vast salt marsh and, like Deal Island, Saxis is a working watermen's town with none of the trappings you might find in a tourist destination. Saxis, and the thousands of acres of marshland around it, is rural and remote, much of it protected as a state Wildlife Management Area. For those of us who enjoy watching wildlife and exploring places that are decidedly off the beaten path, the bays, creeks, and marshes around Saxis can provide many hours of enjoyment.

If you're a fairly experienced paddler, the waters around Saxis are great to explore by canoe or kayak. Brief descriptions of two sample trips follow. If you're more comfortable behind the wheel of a car, by all means get a good map and hit the back roads.

To reach Saxis, travel to Temperanceville on U.S. Route 13, and turn west on state Route 695. This two-lane road will take you through little communities, such as Makemie Park, Grotons, and Sanford. Shortly after passing through Sanford, Route 695 takes a right turn and heads across more than three miles of marsh meadow. It's a beautiful drive, especially late in the day when the sun is beginning to creep toward the horizon and is washing warm light all over that cordgrass. This is Freeschool Marsh, part of the state's Saxis Wildlife Management Area (WMA), a sprawling tract of nearly 6,000 acres that stretches from Pocomoke Sound south to Guard Shore some seven miles away.

There are two basic types of boat trips in the waters near Saxis: open water paddling and creek exploration, also known as "blue lining" because on the topo maps these waterways appear as squiggly blue lines. In general, the trip you decide to take will be determined by the weather and the season.

For example, Guard Shore, on the mainland south of Saxis, offers a long, sandy beach with a gentle berm. To the west is Jobes Island and the open bay. Playing around with the kayak at Guard Shore in July or August would be a refreshing summertime experience, but in the winter it would be foolhardy to plan an open water trip there, especially if the wind is from the northwest and is pushing up a chop across many miles of open bay.

The upper portion of Pitts Creek, on the other hand, is narrow with a wooded shoreline that provides protection from the wind. It is a great place to see wildlife in the fall and winter, but in August, with no breeze, it can be a bit stifling. A modest dose of common sense will help you plan a trip that is comfortable and safe.

Pitts Creek, although not in the Saxis WMA, is one of the most beautiful and intriguing waterways on the Virginia portion of the Eastern Shore, a jewel that is rarely noticed. It begins near the mouth of the Pocomoke River and meanders inland for some ten miles along the Maryland/Virginia line; it is an uncommonly beautiful stream, undeveloped and wild along most of its length. Although its run is rather brief, the creek provides a great example of how waterways and the surrounding landscape change as a river flows inland.

The put-in at the mouth of the creek is a small county boat ramp on the south bank of the Pocomoke River. To get there, take Route 709 west from New Church on U.S. Route 13. Turn right just before the road ends to reach the ramp. If you put a canoe or kayak in here and paddle upstream, you'll find Pitts Creek about a quarter-mile ahead on the right. The creek meanders for some ten miles through salt marsh, forest, hardwood swamp, and farmland, crossing Route 13 just north of the Virginia line at Beaverdam.

Pitts Creek gradually changes from a saltwater creek to a blackwater swamp. Put-in at the boat landing and you'll see marsh grasses and lush wide meadows that run all the way to the pine woods in the distance. For about five miles, the creek flows through this cordgrass swamp. It is a wide, sweeping vista. In the winter, muskrat lodges stand out among the rotting grass. Little open ponds will have black ducks, teal, and shorebirds. Bald eagles can often be seen overhead.

A little farther upstream we find cattails and sedges, providing further evidence that we are leaving a saltwater environment and entering one where freshwater dominates. The bank begins to take on a sturdier, more well-defined edge. Grasses are replaced by shrubs and tall plants called marsh hibiscus, which in the summer has large white and pink blossoms. At about the halfway point the character of Pitts Creek changes completely. The grasses are gone and the landscape makes an incredible transformation into a southern cypress swamp. Bald cypress, cedars, gums, and pines line the shore, standing in shallow freshwater. The creek narrows, the water darkens, and the landscape undergoes a total transformation.

Guard Shore is located on the opposite end of the paddling spectrum. This bayside beach on the mainland, west of the community of Bloxom, has been a popular summer gathering spot for generations. It offers a sandy beach, shallow water, a fairly primitive boat ramp, and great views of salt meadows, offshore islands, and the Chesapeake Bay.

If you've just gotten a new canoe or kayak, this would be a great place to try it out. The best way to learn the limits of a boat is to intentionally tip it. Bring your new craft to Guard Shore when the weather is warm, paddle a few yards offshore, and see what you have to do to swamp it. This little exercise is a great confidence builder when you're just starting out.

Guard Shore was once privately owned, but now is part of the Saxis WMA. Bathing, beachcombing, canoeing and kayaking, fishing, and birding are popular activities. The beach is sandy and narrow, about 1,500 feet long. A rock breakwater separates the beach from the parking area, and the best place to put-in is near the old boat ramp on the northern end of the parking lot. There are no rocks there, just gently sloping sandy beach.

Guard Shore is a narrow ribbon of sand and asphalt fronting the bay. The backside of this little peninsula also offers some paddling opportunities, especially if the breeze is kicking up and you're looking for a protected area. The area is shallow, with several small creeks that wind through the marsh until they become unnavigable.

Great and snowy egrets and great blue herons hunt small fish in the shallows, and you'll likely see ospreys soaring overhead from April through fall. There usually are northern harriers over the high marsh, and bald eagles nest in the area. These shallow waters are also home to diamondback terrapins, which nest on the beach of Guard Shore and other sandy stretches. If you stop paddling and be still for a few minutes, you will likely see some small heads emerge from the calm water. These will be diamondbacks, the only turtle to live in brackish waters.

The Saxis area, for the most part, is rural and remote, great to tour by car or by boat, although it is a bit wild for beginning paddlers. A good introduction to Saxis would be to invest in a topo map of the area or a detailed Accomack County map, and drive the back roads, many of which end at the water's edge.

A number of years ago local historian Kirk Mariner wrote a book about Eastern Shore's back roads called *Off 13*, in which he wrote of Saxis: "Here is a place for those who cherish authenticity; a real, live seafood village well off the beaten path, with not an iota of tourism, and rarely a visitor."

Mariner had it right back then, and Saxis hasn't changed much in the interim.

40

Tangier by Bike

A Boat Ride and a Bike Ride Fueled by a Memorable Lunch

Bike riding is like a religion in that it absolves you of all guilt. I had a friend in college who regularly got wild and crazy on Saturday nights, but on Sunday mornings he was a regular in chapel, a bit bleary eyed and unsteady, but invariably present and repentant.

What brings this to mind is that my son, Tom, and I not long ago took a boat trip to Tangier Island. No, we didn't get wild and crazy — folks don't do that on Tangier — but we did overindulge. We threw aside all restraint and for an hour or so wallowed in unmitigated gluttony, an act that would bring a black cloud of guilt over the head of anyone remotely interested in his cholesterol level.

If you've ever visited the beautiful island of Tangier and stopped for lunch in Crockett's Chesapeake House, you'll know whereof I speak. Meals here are served family-style, in portions designed for men and women who have been on the bay fishing crabpots since dawn. There are crab cakes, clam fritters, baked ham, homemade rolls, corn pudding, green beans, coleslaw, pickled beets, pitchers of iced tea, and thick slabs of pound cake for dessert. Other than the crab cakes (two are served), you are welcome to indulge yourself until a black cloud forms over your head.

Now, about bike riding and religion and how both absolve you of guilt. Tom and I went to Tangier aboard the *Joyce Marie II*, which, during the summer months, sails daily from Onancock. We rode to the Onancock dock on bikes, met Captain Mark Crockett, loaded our bikes onto the *Joyce Marie II*, and sat back to enjoy the hour-and-a-half crossing.

We left Onancock at 10 a.m., with a soft morning haze still hanging over the quiet water. There are a few homes along Onancock Creek — some new and some dating back to the eighteenth century — but no intense development as seen along so much of our coast. There is a sense of history here. Steamboat wharves jutted into the creek in the 1800s and early 1900s. Farmers would bring their produce to the wharves to meet the steamboats, and locally grown potatoes, cabbage, and other crops would be sent to market in Baltimore. Local folks would catch up on news from the big city.

Onancock celebrated its 300th birthday more than twenty years ago, so the town, and the creek that shares its name, have a rich history. Onancock was once the port of

entry for Accomack County, making it a regular call for commercial sailing vessels. Before the railroad came through in 1884, Onancock was the place to go if you wanted to book passage to Baltimore or other Chesapeake Bay destinations. Even after the coming of rail, many travelers still boarded a steamboat in Onancock for business or pleasure travel.

Today, the *Joyce Marie II* is the only passenger vessel that calls here regularly. She was built in Maine in 1988, a lobster boat that frequently is taken for a classic Chesapeake Bay deadrise, and like the deadrise she is able to navigate the shallow waters around Tangier, but is comfortable in a chop crossing Pocomoke Sound. She is thirty-six feet long and Coast Guard-certified for twenty-five passengers.

The passengers these days are a mix of Tangier residents who have come to visit friends or go shopping on the mainland and tourists who have come to enjoy a scenic boat ride highlighted by an island tour and a lunch of fresh seafood and garden vegetables.

As the *Joyce Marie II* neared the mouth of the Onancock Creek, the community of East Point appeared on the south shore and Weir Point and Parker's Marsh, a state natural area preserve, on the north. The channel zigzags through a shoal area here, and nearly all of the red and green channel markers had active osprey nests atop them.

Weir Point, a sandy spit topped by a fringe of saltwater bush, separates the Onancock Creek and Chesapeake Bay. We passed the point, passed the number one channel marker, and were quickly in the bay proper. The flat water gave way to a gentle swell, which the *Joyce Marie II* cut through smoothly, the powerful diesel rumbling confidently below deck.

Uninhabited Watts Island passed on our right, and soon the water tank and church steeple of Tangier came into view. The port is on the north side of the island, and we slowed down and cruised past crab shedding houses on both sides of the channel. Here, freshly caught crabs are packed for market, some to be served as soft crabs, some as steamed, hard crabs, and others to be shelled and sold in pound containers of backfin and special crab meat.

When the boat docked, most of the passengers made their way to Crockett's Chesapeake House or to one of the other island restaurants for lunch. Tom and I climbed aboard our mountain bikes and explored the island streets and pathways.

Tangier is a small island, and you're not going to get an intense workout by pedaling a bike around the town, but biking is a great way to see Tangier. You can start at the boat dock, ride south along the main street, and then cross a bridge and return in a circular route that weaves through residential neighborhoods and crosses a salt marsh. Intersecting with this main circular route are small roads and paths well worth exploring. One path we took ended at a quiet beach, where children were swimming in the bay. It's not a long ride, but it's enough to stretch the legs after a boat ride and work up an appetite.

The reward of exploring the island by bike is that you get to see places that most visitors on foot will miss. Of course, at the end of the ride, you can park the bikes under the shade tree at Chesapeake House, slake your thirst with a glass of iced tea, and then go after those crab cakes and clam fritters with a clear conscience.

41

Onancock by Kayak

Paddling with a Pod of Dolphins

We were drifting along with a pod of bottle-nosed dolphins, amazed that an animal so large could be so graceful. They arched smoothly out of the water, and in the same movement re-entered with hardly a splash. Indeed, they seemed to move with equal comfort through sea and air, traveling in a group of about a dozen.

We were just off Weir Point on the north side of Onancock Creek, where the shipping channel zigzags through sandy shoals as though it had been laid out by an underwater mole with a caffeine overdose. Boat captains have to be on alert when coming and going here — miss one of those red or green navigational aids and you go from a depth of twenty feet to two feet or less, and then comes that sinking feeling of hull plowing sand.

We had little to worry about, though, because we were paddling sea kayaks, trim little sixteen-foot water darts that almost could make way on the morning dew. Your perspective is at just above water level, which makes dolphin-watching especially fun.

Onancock Creek is one of my favorite places to paddle because it presents an unusual combination of history, unspoiled nature, shopping, and wonderful food. In a leisurely day, you can put-in at the town harbor, paddle out to Weir Point (where the creek meets the Chesapeake Bay), and finish the trip with a dinner of fresh soft crabs, or perhaps a medley of local seafood in a cream sauce served over pasta.

The town of Onancock (o-NAN-cock) celebrated its 300th birthday more than twenty years ago, so the community has a storied past, most of which is centered around its deep water port. In 1680, the Virginia General Assembly declared Onancock a port of entry for Accomack County, and approximately fifty acres between two forks of the creek were purchased from Charles Scarburgh, for whom the community was briefly named.

Farmers brought their crops to the Onancock Wharf to be sent to market, and they came to Onancock to pick up goods and supplies. First came the sailing ships and later the steamers, which linked Onancock with Norfolk, Baltimore, and other ports along the bay.

There still is evidence of this history at the Onancock Wharf. Hopkins and Bro. General Store was the hub of the shipping business in the nineteenth century, and today is a restaurant. A walk up Market Street will take you to historic Ker Place (circa 1797), a museum, and the headquarters for the Eastern Shore of Virginia Historical Society.

Slip your kayak or canoe into Onancock Creek and more history unfolds. A short distance out the creek are numerous old homes, some of which were the sites of plantations during the days when Onancock was the port of entry. Finney's Wharf, on the south side of the creek, was another steamboat stop. On the opposite side of the creek, a little farther west, is Only Point, the site of an historic home built in 1843 by Henry A. Wise, who served as governor of Virginia from 1855 to 1859. The house is not typical of Eastern Shore architecture; the late historian Ralph Whitelaw speculated that it was designed by a Philadelphia architect employed by Wise's wife, who was from the north.

Farther out the creek, and on the opposite shore, is Bailey Neck and the home, Baliwick. This area is still, for the most part, a working farm, where corn and soybeans are grown for market. Across the creek is Poplar Cove, another creekside village that years ago was a commercial port and a harbor for commercial watermen.

At Bailey Point, the creek widens and the bay comes into view. Several smaller creeks (Finneys, Parkers) break off from the main channel along the southern shore, and on the north is Parker's Marsh Natural Area Preserve, a vast cordgrass meadow with lots of winding channels that beg exploring. Weir Point on the northern bank and Thicket Point on the south mark the junction of the bay and the creek.

While the creekside farms nearer the town offer reminders of the history of the area, Parker's Marsh Natural Area Preserve is where you want to go to see wildlife and to experience the creek as it might have been before Onancock became a port of entry. The shallow tidal waterways have waterfowl in the fall and winter, as well as a variety of wading birds, such as herons and egrets. Ospreys nest on channel markers, and clapper rails can be heard in the marsh.

It's approximately ten miles round-trip from the Onancock Wharf to Weir Point, but given that most people rarely paddle kayaks and canoes in a straight line, add a few more miles to that and explore some offshoots of Onancock Creek, such as Leatherbury Branch, Cedar Creek, and the meandering, unnamed waterways of Parker's Marsh Natural Area Preserve.

Onancock Creek is protected by a forested shoreline for much of its distance, so wind is not usually a factor, especially when paddling the upper portions of the creek. The creek widens considerably beyond Bailey Point, however, and at times can be rough, especially if the wind is from the west or southwest.

The creek is relatively shallow outside the marked channel, with depths perhaps two to six feet. We stay in the shallow water, closer to land, because there's a great deal more wildlife to see in this edge where land meets water, and we prefer to avoid motorboat traffic. Being in a channel in a small boat, with a large powerboat bearing down on you, can definitely give you the feeling of being a target.

A paddling trip on Onancock Creek can't be complete without also taking a walking tour of the town. In addition to Hopkins Store and Ker Place, there are art galleries, antique and gift shops, a theater, and probably more restaurants per capita than any town in Virginia. Onancock's population is around 1,500, and there are at least ten restaurants, with a menu ranging from cold-cuts to caviar.

For more formal dining, there are a number of choices: small restaurants with a European flair, a wine bar, and waterfront eateries that specialize in local seafood. Somehow that makes kayaking Onancock Creek even more pleasurable, knowing that at day's end your reward might be some fresh seafood taken from the very waters you spent the day sharing with dolphins.

42

Folly Creek Clam Chowder
In Search of Mercenaria

Soup companies would have us believe that there are two kinds of clam chowder: New England, which is creamy, and Manhattan, which is tomatoey. Those of us who live on Delmarva, especially on the seaside of Delmarva, know this is a crock.

Our clam chowder has clams and potatoes, perhaps a little onion, perhaps bits of bacon, and little else. New Englanders can keep their cream. As for Manhattan, well, I'd be disinclined to eat a clam that came from waters anywhere near there.

Our clam chowder is made with salty, seaside hardshell clams, *Mercenaria mercenaria*, so named because Native Americans made beads from the blue inner shells and used these beads in trade, wampum. You can find clams most anywhere on Delmarva where there is saltwater and tidal flats, from Delaware Bay to the Virginia Capes. At Assateague National Seashore, they give lessons in clamming during the summer.

Clams burrow just beneath the surface of the flat, and when the flat is exposed at low tide, you can find the small holes, or strings of waste, where the clam's siphons extended to the surface. This evidence of the presence of a clam is called "sign," which is both a noun and a verb, e.g. "The clams are signing good today."

I grew up near Folly Creek and often would go clamming with my father and his friends. He would take along a bushel basket placed inside an inflated tire tube and he would fasten this float to his waist with string. He would dig clams using a special rake with long tines, and he would pry them from the tidal flat, rinse them in seawater, and place them in the basket. If the clamming was good, the basket would be filled in a little over an hour.

One of the pleasures of clamming is that it is one of the few outdoor sports to have been tread upon lightly by government regulators. There are no seasons, no license requirement for recreational clamming, and the bag limit is a downright generous, 250 per person, which translates to a lot of chowder.

Nor is clamming a socially demanding sport. There is no proper clamming attire; I wear hip boots in cold weather and shorts in the summer. You won't find graphite-shafted clamming picks in the Orvis® catalog. There are no clamming magazines to subscribe to or non-profit organizations whose noble goal it is to save the clam.

All you need to go clamming is a convenient tidal flat in saltwater, old sneakers or water shoes to protect the feet, and an instrument to dislodge the clam once you find it. Most sporting goods and hardware stores in coastal communities sell clam picks or clam rakes. A clam rake resembles the garden variety except that it has longer tines, which are handy for prying the clam loose. Rakes are used in shallow water where you can't see the clam holes, or sign, and they can be used on exposed flats when the clams are not signing.

If I'm in a hurry for clam chowder, or on days when I don't have the patience to look for clam sign, I'll take the rake along and simply drag it across the flat, hoping for the familiar scrape of metal against shell. This is clamming at its unsophisticated low mark — sort of like fishing for carp under the railroad bridge compared to casting dry flies for native trout in a mountain stream — but it is effective.

Our favorite method is signing and our favorite time to go clamming is in late fall, when the flounder fishermen have left, the winter birds are arriving, and we usually have the tidal flats to ourselves. Lynn and I took off one recent afternoon to explore Folly Creek, which begins near the town of Accomac and flows eastward, where it empties into Metompkin Inlet, which separates Metompkin and Cedar Islands. It was cold, but not numbingly so, and there is no wide water to cross on Folly Creek, which makes it a relatively safe waterway for winter boating.

It was low tide in early afternoon, and our intention was to explore the creek, look for birds, and then end the trip by picking up some shellfish on a tidal flat to take home and have for dinner. We saw only two other boats that day, a well-worn scow used by a local waterman who was searching for oysters in the marsh, and the other a duck hunters' boat that had been covered with cedar boughs and looked something like a floating Christmas tree waiting for ornaments.

As we headed out the creek, little bufflehead ducks flew off in front of us, just a foot or two off the surface of the water. These little birds are the signal that winter has arrived. They are handsome characters, the drakes rather dapper with striking white flanks and a white patch on the head. Now, they travel in loose flocks of perhaps a dozen birds, but by late winter the creeks will be filled with them; rafts of fifty or one hundred ducks will part as your boat goes through and then reconvene a short distance away.

We saw loons, herons, and heard clapper rails calling in the high marsh. North of us, probably near the northern end of Metompkin Island, snow geese were scattered along the horizon like low clouds. There must have been thousands of them. Now and then we could hear the muffled bump of a distant shotgun.

As low tide drew near, Lynn and I pulled the boat onto a tidal flat. With full moon, the tide was exceptionally low, and we had close to one hundred acres to explore. At one end of the flat is a bed of oyster shells, and among them we found shrimp and spiny urchins. Whelks had burrowed beneath the surface, and the flat was covered with holes left by worms and various crustaceans.

The surface of the flat, although wet and slick, was firm in most places, with mud and sand tightly packed by the pressure of the water at high tide. We wore knee boots and walked about easily, prying out interesting shells and watching the shorebirds gathering in the distance.

We had hoped to find clams for dinner, and we brought the clam picks and a basket. Just as the tide began to rise, the clams began to sign, and we picked up several dozen. A high marsh joins the tidal flat, and walking along this edge I found clusters of oysters and mussels. These went into the basket with the clams, but not before I opened a few of the oysters and had them on the spot, sweet and very salty, the taste of the ocean that was crashing on the beach a few hundred yards away.

Back at home, we opened the clams, chopped them coarsely, and began our chowder. We first fried bacon, which was set aside for tomorrow's breakfast. We then sautéed chopped potatoes and onion in the bacon grease until they were just brown, and we added the clam juice to deglaze the pan. We cooked the potatoes and onions until they were just done, and then we added the chopped clams, cooking them through but not to the point that they would become tough. We added a little ground black pepper, but nothing else — no tomatoes and no cream. It's not New England, and it's not Manhattan. Let's call it Folly Creek clam chowder.

43

Surf Fishing on the Barrier Beaches

The Best Place on Delmarva Not to Catch Fish

If you must go fishing and not catch fish, the best place to do so is in the surf of the barrier islands that line Virginia's Eastern Shore. What we have here is the last of the coastal wilderness on the Mid-Atlantic, miles and miles of uninterrupted beach — no roads, no parking lots, no dunes sculpted by bulldozers — just nature in its original configuration.

As with many wilderness areas, these islands are not easy to get to. You can't take a bus or drive your car. You have to go by boat, which means you either have to know the water or go with someone who does. Nature-oriented tourism has taken hold on Virginia's Eastern Shore in recent years, and several companies offer day-trips to the islands and many of the tour operators are willing to take you fishing. Contact the local chambers of commerce for details.

I grew up near Folly Creek, so I can find my way out the creek to Cedar Island fairly easily. Lynn and I recently took advantage of a spectacular late fall Saturday to go surf fishing on the north end of this barrier beach. We were hoping to catch a channel bass, or perhaps a black drum, as they migrated south along the coast, but we took chicken breasts out of the freezer before leaving, just in case we came home with nothing more than leftover bait and a sunburn.

Surf fishing is like playing poker. You know you're probably going to leave your money on the table, but you go anyway, because there is a chance of success, and because in the past you've been successful just often enough to make you a believer.

Surf fishing also is an excuse to do something most sane people would not. On a crisp fall day, sweater weather, I took off my shoes, stripped down to my shorts, and waded out, first knee-deep, and then after a breaker caught me, waist-deep. I stood there for two hours, now and then retreating to the beach for more bait, and watched the surf, felt the pull of the undertow stealing the sand from beneath my feet, and wished to be no place else.

The power of the surf is mesmerizing, especially when you're standing in it, trying to cast a bait far enough beyond the breakers to reach a shallow slough where a channel bass could be foraging. I think of it as high sensory fishing. The ocean is at first alarmingly cold, but then you become used to it and get comfortable. The sand moves under your feet as you crunch your way through a shell bed, and there is the unending tumble of white water, creating a sound that is loud and constant, yet very pleasing and natural.

You don't experience these things when you're bottom fishing for croakers.

As Lynn and I fished, ragged flocks of cormorants made their way along the beach, just beyond the surf line. Brown pelicans glided and dove, coming down in a crash we couldn't hear above the surf sound. Behind us, black ducks flew over the salt marsh, searching for shallow ponds and guts in which to feed. They reminded me that our son, Tom, and I need to brush up the duck blind before the season begins.

Lynn and I had the beach to ourselves. As far as we could see, in any direction, there were no other people — only miles of surf, a broad expanse of sand and shell, thousands of acres of tidal marsh, and, in the distance, the mainland.

The only immediate evidence of humans was the old Coast Guard station that sits in the marsh on the north end of the island. The station was abandoned in the 1960s and is weathered to various shades of gray. Unlike some beach houses, it is part of the landscape, and has been for years. Between the surf and the old station is a low dune line where seaside goldenrod grows in thick beds in late fall. Both the goldenrod and the station seem to belong here.

Lynn and I shared the beach with several species of gulls, ring-bills just moving in for the winter, and laughing gulls in the process of moving to more southerly shores. There were also sanderlings, which would race the waves in and out, foraging amid the froth left by the surf.

Sanderlings are nervous little birds, constantly in motion, as if they had stayed a little too long at the coffee bar. Because they burn so many calories, they have to feed constantly. It seems this bird has gotten itself onto a vicious treadmill. It must run in order to feed and it must feed in order to run.

We had launched our little skiff from a public boat ramp nearby and had made our way to the island through several miles of salt marsh channels. We beached the boat, loaded bait, tackle, and lunch into daypacks, and hiked across the island to the surf. It's more work than driving your 4x4 to the beach, but the wildness is worth it.

Most of these islands are owned either by The Nature Conservancy, the state, or are protected as federal wildlife refuge. It's pleasing to know that this coastal wilderness will remain wild and that our grandchildren and their grandchildren will be able to wade in the surf, cast a bait to channel bass, and enjoy the experience so thoroughly they don't need to bring home fish to make the day a success.

44

Bottom Bouncing on the Bay

In Search of "A Nice Mess of Fish"

One thing most Delmarva communities have in common is proximity to saltwater, meaning ample opportunity to catch "a nice mess of fish," which very likely is a term that is Delmarva's own. At least I've never heard it used elsewhere. A nice mess of fish indicates no exact number, but is widely understood to imply both quantity and quality.

Some types of fishing are very focused. In the fall, we cast lures for rockfish, or we use tiny pieces of clam around buoys to entice spadefish, or we cast baits of clam or peeler crab in barrier island surf in hopes of landing a channel bass.

To catch a nice mess of fish we go out in open water, anchor or drift over areas we know to be productive, and fish on the bottom, with a two-hook rig with just enough weight to keep it stable in the current. For bait, we use slices of squid, perhaps a minnow, a bloodworm, or a piece of peeler crab if any can be found. We don't know what we're going to catch, and that makes bottom fishing fun.

The goal is to come home with a nice mess of fish, and in the olden days, before size restrictions and bag limits, this meant enough to have for dinner, a few for the freezer, and some for neighbors who enjoy eating fish, but don't get to go fishing that often. Keeper size was usually determined by whether the fish was big enough to filet.

We do most of our bottom fishing on the Chesapeake Bay, and this usually means taking the boat out of Onancock Creek to an area called Ditchbank, a few miles from the mouth of the creek. Ditchbank is an underwater river, where the depth drops from a steady twenty feet to more than fifty feet in a relatively short distance. We fish along the drop-off, usually in about thirty-five feet of water. We found an old shellbed along the slope, and when we anchor over it, we usually catch fish. Now and then, we'll hook an ancient shell and bring it up, and in large ones we'll find small crabs, shrimp, and other crustaceans, so we know why larger fish tend to hang out on the bottom around shellbeds.

Most people who live along the Chesapeake, or, for that matter, along the bays and creeks of the seaside, have favorite fishing spots such as this, places that have consistently produced nice messes of fish. When we bottom fish, we might catch croakers, gray trout, bluefish, flounder, sand mullet, and, in late summer, spot and pigfish. Pigfish are small panfish that are beautifully colored when they just come out of the water. They snort and grunt like a pig, hence the name. Like spot, they are excellent when fried and served with cornbread, butterbeans, and stewed tomatoes. It's not a dish you'll find on many restaurant menus, but a seasonal favorite in most communities along the bay.

Swelling toads also are caught frequently and make a wonderful seafood dish. Swelling toads also are known as blow toads, and, by seafood marketing types, as sea squab. To clean toads, you slice into the skin just behind the head, pull the skin away, and remove the firm, white tenderloin of fish. Most people fry them as they would any other panfish, but our favorite recipe, and I'm not making this up, is toad kebabs. We use small toads, marinate them as we would shrimp, and put them on skewers with mushrooms, pineapple chunks, sweet peppers, and tomatillos or other firm vegetables. The mixture is cooked over charcoal and served with brown rice.

The mess of fish we bring home varies with the season, and with the inevitable population swings of various species. As this is being written, a mess of fish will be dominated by croakers. Indeed, many fishermen report catches of a "nice mess of croakers," meaning croakers of nice size, but very little else.

Croakers are unappreciated by many, but when they're in great numbers, as they have been in recent years, they provide consistent fishing in most of the waters that surround Delmarva. They can be caught from boats, from piers, and even by casting from docks and bridges, if fishing is allowed.

Croakers are also underestimated as table fare. Try fileting them, basting with a little mayonnaise, dusting with Cajun season, and broiling until just done, or try croakers done caveman-style. Leave the fish whole, slit it from throat to vent, remove the innards, and cook it unscaled over charcoal. Pick out the tender white meat with a fork, and serve it with a little butter and lemon juice and your favorite seafood seasoning.

Our family enjoys occasional trips to the mountains, and one of the hotels where we stay features a Friday evening seafood buffet, a big hit among people who live in the area and who crowd the restaurant on Friday nights. There are snow crab legs, farm-raised salmon filets dyed orange, tilapia in tomato and pepper sauce, clam strips, both Manhattan and New England clam chowder, steamed shrimp, and breaded, fried fish of undetermined origin. Unknown to them are pan-fried pigfish, caveman croakers, or toad kebabs. They have no concept of what a nice mess of fish might include. Just as well. We'll keep it our little Delmarva-lous secret.

The Eastern Shore
Barrier Islands Center

Virginia's Focal Point for Barrier Island History

Virginia's Eastern Shore has a national natural treasure, a string of twenty-three barrier islands that for the most part are as they were when the first blue-eyed British dandy arrived in 1607. What we have here is the last of the coastal wilderness: open beaches that stretch uninterrupted for miles, thousands of acres of salt meadow, meandering tidal creeks winding their way into upland forests, and shallow bays that are prolific breeding grounds for many species of fish and shellfish.

Virginia's barrier beaches are remote, accessible only by boat, and even then visitors must know what they're doing. This difficulty of access has contributed to the islands' lack of development over the years, and it makes them special places. There are few stretches quite like this anywhere on the Mid-Atlantic Coast: no hotels, no restaurants, no towns, no roads, and no souvenir shops — nothing but nature at her wildest and best.

Most of the islands on the Virginia coast are owned by The Nature Conservancy and are protected as the Virginia Coast Reserve, a sanctuary of more than 40,000 acres. The conservancy allows day use of its island property, but that still doesn't solve the problem of getting there. The bays and creeks that separate the islands from the mainland are shallow and filled with dangerous oyster reefs. Storms can also whip up these waters in a hurry and folks who are not familiar with the area can get in trouble very easily.

A solution would be to book a trip with one of the nature-oriented tourism companies on the Eastern Shore (local chambers of commerce and tourism offices have information), or you could have an island experience on the mainland in the little village of Machipongo, just off Route 13.

The Eastern Shore of Virginia Barrier Islands Center is located on an eighteen-acre working farm in a rambling frame building that more than a century ago was called the Almshouse, a facility to house the poor. The building and other structures on the farm were vacant for many years, but in 2002 a group of local residents opened the facility as the home of the barrier islands center, an organization formed in the 1990s to help preserve island history and artifacts. Until 2002, the center had no permanent home, but when renovation of the old buildings began, and when artifacts began arriving, the Almshouse Farm became a focal point for the history and culture of the barrier islands and the rural Eastern Shore.

"We're two museums in one," said director Laura Vaughan. "We interpret the life of a working farm as it might have been more than a century ago, and we are a museum of the history and culture of the Virginia barrier islands. We have eighteen acres, which are still under cultivation, and we have three buildings that are on the National Register of Historic Places. The large building is where the poor white people were housed, another housed poor blacks, and a third is a 1725 kitchen building that is remarkably intact."

This colorful history, tragic in a way, yet hopeful in that the community did provide for its less-fortunate residents, can be seen in the many artifacts that fill the rooms where residents once slept and ate their meals. It is a history not only of these residents, but of people who lived an entirely different life several miles away, in villages on Cobb's Island and Hog Island, in lifesaving stations on Metompkin and Parramore, and in lavish sporting clubs, such as the Accomack Club, that once stood in the marshes between Wachapreague and Parramore Island.

At the end of the nineteenth century, several hundred people lived on the barrier islands, in small villages, such as Broadwater, on Hog Island, or on Assateague, across the channel from Chincoteague. On other islands there were temporary living quarters, encampments basically, where mainland residents pastured their livestock. Hunting clubs and hotels were on several islands, perhaps the most famous being the Cobb family retreat that catered to hunters and fishermen from around the country. Another hotel was on Wallops Island, where today NASA has a rocket launch facility.

The human presence on the islands probably was at a peak in the late nineteenth and early twentieth centuries. Island people lived off the land and the sea, catching crabs, clams, fish, and oysters that were taken to the mainland to be shipped to market. In winter, local men guided visiting hunters, and until laws were passed making market gunning illegal, they killed waterfowl and shipped them to clients in northern cities.

Many island residents realized in the early 1900s that their way of life was threatened. The Cobb hotel was destroyed by a storm, and most realized that the sea level was rising. The crushing blow came in 1933, when a strong storm wreaked havoc on the East Coast. Houses were flooded, lives were lost, and many people made plans to evacuate. Over the years, homes in the village of Broadwater were loaded onto barges, ferried across the bay to the mainland, and were rebuilt in mainland towns, such as Willis Wharf, Wachapreague, and Oyster.

By the middle part of the 1900s, the only permanent human presence on the islands was the Coast Guard, which had stations on most of the barrier beaches. By the 1960s, though, modern technology was making these outposts obsolete. Radio communication, high-speed boats and aircraft, and the development of radar and GPS made human presence on each island unnecessary. Parramore became the final island station to close in the 1990s.

With the human presence on the islands coming to an end, several residents of the Eastern Shore became alarmed that many of the artifacts associated with island life were leaving the area and that this connection to the history and culture of the Shore was being lost. A group, headed by artist Thelma Peterson, formed a non-profit organization to protect these remnants of island life. Over the years the group grew and funds were raised. The high-mark came when the doors of Almshouse Farm opened to the public in 2002.

A visit to the museum cannot replace an actual visit to one of these wild barrier beaches, but an afternoon there can provide a feeling for what life might have been like when the workday revolved around the rising and falling of the tides and when the paycheck was as uncertain as nature itself.

Savage Neck Dunes

A Remote and Ancient Landscape on the Bay

Not so long ago, people who lived in the southern part of Delmarva used to gather at a remote, hilly area on the shore of the Chesapeake Bay near the Northampton County town of Eastville. At that time, the place was called Sand Hills, aptly named because of the extensive system of secondary dunes that ran parallel to the shoreline of the Chesapeake Bay. People picnicked there, had hay rides, and rumor has it that young people might have participated in late-night parties at Sand Hills.

Among local folks, especially those of a certain age, the area is still called Sand Hills and forever will be, but Sand Hills now is owned by the state as a natural area preserve and the official title is Savage Neck Dunes.

The name has changed, but the landscape has not. These dunes are unique along the Chesapeake Bay, rising a lofty fifty feet above sea level, covered with stunted loblolly pines and wild black cherry, patches of beach heather here and there along the slopes.

The state was interested in the site because it is home to a threatened species, the northeastern beach tiger beetle, and because of the unique geological feature of the dunes and the plant and animal communities they support.

"The farmland and dunes were purchased from private landowners in 1998 and 1999," said Dot Field, Eastern Shore region steward with the state Department of Conservation and Recreation Division of Natural Heritage. "We have 298 acres and a mile of shoreline along the Chesapeake. It's important because it's great tiger beetle habitat, but it also is prime habitat for migrating songbirds."

Dot Field and I met in a small parking lot maintained by the state along Route 634, east of the town of Eastville. We walked along a grassy path that led from the parking area, along a former farm field, to a freshwater pond, and finally into a maritime forest, where there were strikingly tall dunes, most of them topped by wind-pruned pine trees and stunted sweet gums.

"This was farmland before the state got it," she explained. "We're managing it now for songbirds, so the fields have reverted to grasslands and shrub thickets. It's a great place to see grasshopper sparrows. The pond has herons and egrets, and wood ducks nest here in the spring."

As we walked along, a belted kingfisher flew over, chattering loudly and a green heron stalked small fish along the shallow shoreline. From the pond, we took a trail through the woods, and soon the ground became sandy and the topography began to change. We then were looking at fifty-foot dunes that spread through the forest as far as we could see.

"These are Holocene-era dunes, probably 10,000 years old," said Field. "This is the highest point on the Eastern Shore of Virginia. It's a huge secondary dune ridge, and today it's pretty much the way it's always been. We were lucky to get it when we did, considering the pressure for development along the bay. There are very few places like this. It's a relic dune system that at one time in its past fronted either the ocean or the bay."

We crossed the secondary dunes, the smaller primary dunes, and then there was the bay stretched out before us, with little sandbars showing here and there at low tide and a white speck of a sailboat in the distance. We looked north and then south. We could see no other people, and very few of the trappings of humans. Only the roof of a small cabin was visible in the woods north of the preserve. "It's pretty amazing to have this much undeveloped land along the bay," said Field. "There are very few places these days where you can stand on a sandy bayside beach and not see homes and other development. The preserve runs for a mile along the bay, so we know this place will be here for future generations to enjoy."

Savage Neck Dunes Natural Area Preserve is not a huge tract, especially when compared to public lands in western Virginia, but it packs a tremendous amount of habitat diversity into less than three hundred acres. Farmland has given way to grasslands and scrub, and old fields are being colonized by sweet gum, the beginning a planned process of forest succession that will last for years. In the summer and fall, the grasslands are filled with butterflies and dragonflies, which breed in the nearby pond. The scrub thickets provide food and shelter to migrating birds and residents alike, and the shallow pond has largemouth bass, bluegill sunfish, black crappie, and many species of amphibians.

A walk through an old mixed forest takes the visitor to the Chesapeake Bay, where the endangered tiger beetles can be seen during warm weather. In the winter, the dunes provide a dramatic vista of the open bay. There will be rafts of surf scoters offshore, perhaps red-breasted merganser diving in the shallows, followed by hovering Bonaparte's gulls, and huge, white northern gannets can be seen diving offshore. It is truly a spectacular place in any season.

Savage Neck Dunes is part of a comprehensive conservation puzzle in Northampton County. The area is vital to migrating birds, which gather by the thousands in the forests and shrub thickets before making the seventeen-mile crossing of the Chesapeake Bay.

It is only one part of a conservation plan that federal, state, and private conservation groups have designed to maintain as much natural land here as possible.

Fisherman Island, at the very tip of the peninsula, is a national wildlife refuge. Eastern Shore of Virginia National Wildlife Refuge is on the mainland at the northern terminus of the Chesapeake Bay Bridge-Tunnel. Kiptopeke State Park is just south of Savage Neck on the bay. Other parcels are owned either by the state or The Nature Conservancy, which has more than 40,000 acres along the Virginia barrier islands.

The future of Savage Neck Dunes seems pretty much secure. It's a haven for wildlife and a beautiful place for a hike, and, as in the past, humans fit into the equation. People are welcome to visit, on foot, and stroll over to the beach and marvel at this unique geological relic. You can even have a picnic, and those of us of a certain age will be forgiven if we slip up and refer to the place as Sand Hills.

47

Fishing on the Dock of a Bay

What to Do When You're Without a Boat

The family wants to catch a few fish, but you don't have a boat and you don't have the cash to book a charter. Not a problem. There are several fishing piers on Delmarva, not to mention public docks, creek banks, and other access points where the fishing is free, or nearly so.

Perhaps the best-known local pier is the Seagull Pier on the Chesapeake Bay Bridge-Tunnel, the seventeen-mile span linking Delmarva with points south. While the substantive toll may make it seem a little expensive to go pier fishing, if you have three or four people in your vehicle, the cost becomes nominal. Besides, where else can you spend the entire day fishing in the middle of the Chesapeake Bay and the only cost is the toll over the bridge?

Many of the boat launch facilities on Delmarva have docks where non-boaters can fish or crab. The Morley's Wharf ramp outside Exmore, Virginia, is a good example.

One of the nicest piers is at Kiptopeke State Park, just north of the Chesapeake Bay Bridge-Tunnel, right on the bay. My son, Tom, and I recently drove down to the park, wanting to catch a few fish, but lacking the time and motivation to launch the boat, gas it up, and go through all the protocol that's attached to the process. We just wanted to fish for a couple of hours, maybe catch a few to have for dinner, and then go home.

We stopped at a local bait shop, bought a half-pound of their smallest shrimp, and drove to the park with our tackle in the back of the truck. Fishing is not free at Kiptopeke, but it's not exactly onerous either, and they have a nice facility with fish-cleaning stations, picnic tables, a gazebo, and a great view of the southern Chesapeake Bay. They charged $3 to park the truck and $3 each to fish from the pier.

For those of us of a certain age, Kiptopeke will be remembered as the ferry terminal, which, until the Chesapeake Bay Bridge-Tunnel opened in 1964, is where you would go to catch a boat for Little Creek and the Tidewater area. The ferry terminal stood on the site of what now is the fishing pier. The cluster of pilings roped together about one hundred and fifty feet off the pier was used to guide ferries into their slip. Farther out, nine World War II vintage concrete ships are lashed together bow to stern to form a breakwater. The breakwater has done its job over the last half-century or more. If you look north and south, you'll see that the shoreline has retreated eastward. Behind the breakwater, the shoreline has held its own, so the fishing pier is like a little finger of land that juts out into the bay.

Pier fishing is convenient in that the truck was parked a short walk from where we fished. When we were ready for a sandwich and soda, lunch was readily at hand and, unlike fishing from a boat, pier fishing is a social occasion. Even if the other people fishing are total strangers, we greet each other, acknowledge catches, share fishing information, and actually form some kind of fleeting kinship.

When Tom and I were fishing, a family from New York was next to us along the railing. Things were quiet until the six-year-old boy hooked a flounder at the very base of the pier. After a brief struggle and excited instructions by the father and uncle, the flounder came over the rail, flopping on the walkway, as a breathless blonde kid jumped up and down. His dad got out the cell phone to call mom, who was back in the campground.

The flounder was more than twenty inches long, well over the minimum size limit, and it quickly drew a crowd. Another shaggy-haired blonde, about four years hold, brought over a saltwater fishing guide published by the state, just in case identification was needed. "I caught one like it last week," he said. "They are very tasty."

Within a few minutes, they went back to their fishing stations. All of us were, perhaps, a little more intent on what we were doing, thinking of a dinner of broiled flounder, new potatoes, and sweet corn. None of us fished with more determination, however, than the six-year old who had brought in the flounder minutes before. In a brief moment on a fishing pier, he became a fisherman for life.

As for Tom and me, as the day wore down, we resigned ourselves to roast beef for dinner, and there's nothing wrong with that. We caught a small croaker and a nice sand mullet that would go into the freezer until reinforcements arrived, and we had a fine afternoon of fishing without the expense and hassle of the boat. We fished with a few kindred spirits and we watched a young person become hooked on fishing.

48

Kiptopeke State Park

A Magnet for Birds and Birders

Northampton County is at the very tip of the Delmarva Peninsula, a narrow ribbon of land separating the Chesapeake Bay from the Atlantic Ocean. Kiptopeke State Park is on the bay, just a few miles north of the tip of the peninsula. Stand on the fishing pier at the park and you can see the Chesapeake Bay Bridge-Tunnel, which connects Delmarva with Tidewater. The bridge-tunnel opened in 1964; prior to that ferries used to dock at Kiptopeke to transport cars, trucks, and passengers across the mouth of the bay to Little Creek. When you stand on the fishing pier, you're standing on the site of the old ferry terminal. Just offshore is a breakwater of nine World War II vintage concrete troop ships, lined bow to stern, to protect the harbor from the open waters of the bay.

When Kiptopeke was a link in the regional transportation system, it supported motels, restaurants, gas stations, and other businesses that provided services to travelers. One of the most prominent motels was the Tourinns Motor Court, which sat high on a hill on the south side of the road, overlooking the ferry terminal. One fall day in 1963, a group of birdwatchers was having lunch at the motel restaurant when they looked out the window and noticed a remarkable number of birds outside. After eating, they picked up their binoculars and began to explore the woods, fields, and dune thickets behind the ferry terminal.

These birdwatchers realized that the birds they were seeing — warblers, tanagers, vireos, thrushes — were migrating south and were gathering here at the tip of the Eastern Shore peninsula before making the eighteen-mile flight over open water to the southern shore of the bay — and they had an idea. What if they were to set up a banding station here in the fall, record the number of species, and begin collecting data that could be used to study the movement of songbirds up and down the east coast?

They did just that, and their lunchtime idea eventually gave ornithologists a half-century of data on the fall migration of songbirds along the East Coast. The original banding station began as a modest operation run by six volunteer birders: Fred Scott,

Charlie Hacker, Mike and Dorothy Mitchell, and Walter and Doris Smith. Today, with the backing of several state and private groups, the station is operated by the Coastal Virginia Wildlife Observatory (CVWO), and the mission of the organization has grown to include a variety of education and research programs.

The banding project pioneered in 1963 ended in 2012, but the organization now operates a hawk observatory each fall and has staff on hand to explain the importance of Kiptopeke in both hawk and songbird migration. In addition, native plant gardens attract a wide variety of butterflies, including migrating monarchs. The Kiptopeke Hawkwatch runs each fall, from September through November, and a monarch butterfly tagging and census runs roughly during the same period.

CVWO recently began a program called Baywatch, which monitors waterbird migration down the Chesapeake Bay shoreline in the fall. The program is being conducted at Pickett's Harbor Natural Area Preserve, a new state-owned protected area just south of Kiptopeke State Park.

When the six birdwatchers interrupted their lunch at the Tourinns Motor Court in 1963 to look for warblers, it began a public realization of how important the Kiptopeke area is to migrating birds and butterflies. The six friends were not aware of it at the time, but they were likely the first to kick off what became a Southern Tip initiative in Northampton County. As state, federal, and private conservation organizations became aware of the importance of the tip, efforts began to protect land there.

Fort John Custis, later known as Cape Charles Air Force Station, was eventually to become the Eastern Shore of Virginia National Wildlife Refuge, protecting the very tip of the peninsula. Later, Fisherman Island, just offshore, also became part of the refuge. In 2002, Virginia voters overwhelmingly approved the State Parks and Natural Area bond referendum, which provided $119 million for new state parks and natural area preserves. A good portion of the funding was used to protect tracts at or near the southern tip and the migratory corridors farther north.

The state added on to Kiptopeke State Park and created natural area preserves at Savage Neck Dunes north of Kiptopeke, protecting a mile of Chesapeake's shoreline, as well as Pickett's Harbor, just south of the park. On the seaside, a large tract known as the Bull Farm, was purchased just north of the wildlife refuge, creating what now is Magothy Bay Natural Area Preserve. A smaller preserve was created on the bay near the town of Cape Charles, suitably named the Cape Charles Natural Area Preserve.

While the federal and state governments were creating wildlife refuges, state parks, and natural area preserves, private conservation interests also were at work. The Nature Conservancy began buying barrier islands and adjacent mainland properties in the early 1970s and later expanded its interest to include islands and saltmarsh tracts on the Chesapeake Bay.

The result, over the years, was a conservation effort by numerous partners that protected one of the most fragile and vulnerable coastal ecosystems along the Mid-

Atlantic — and it began with six amateur birdwatchers stopping for lunch at Tourinns Restaurant before boarding the ferry for the trip across the bay.

If you visit the hawkwatch platform at Kiptopeke State Park, high on an old dune overlooking the harbor, take a glance at the shrub thicket just north of the platform, near the remains of an old driveway. There, amid the cedars and wax myrtle, is a bit of rusted, weathered metal that has something of an *arts nouveau* sculptural quality. Four metal squares are arranged on the edge, supported by two upright posts. The squares are faded, but at one time must have been glossy red, yellow, and black. Across them, in large letters once lit by neon, are the words "Tourinns Motor Court." Attached to them is a smaller sign in red and white. "Free TV," it reads.

If you stand on the platform at Kiptopeke and witness the flight of passing hawks or see warblers feeding on the seeds of wax myrtle shrubs, keep in mind that something rather remarkable began here. There were six friends who shared an interest in birds, and as they ate lunch, they looked out the window of the Tourinns Restaurant, and they had an idea.

49

Fisherman Island

This Time We're Not Just Passing Through

What island on Delmarva gets thousands of visitors daily, yet few people actually set foot on it? The answer would be Fisherman Island, that oasis of sand, salt marsh, and tidal flats at the very southern tip of the Delmarva Peninsula.

Cars, trucks, and motorcycles constantly zip across the island, but they're just passing through, heading either to Hampton Roads and points south or heading north on U.S. Route 13 up the Delmarva Peninsula. Fisherman Island is protected as a national wildlife refuge, and those inviting sandy beaches, grassy dunes, and tidal flats are all off-limits. You can look, but you can't touch.

Fisherman Island National Wildlife Refuge is a vital nesting area for many species of birds, notably the royal tern and brown pelican, which nest in colonies of thousands each spring and summer. The refuge is closed so that these birds, and others, may go about their business uninterrupted by human interference.

Once the birds have nested and are on their way south for the winter, though, then you may get a little Fisherman Island sand between your toes and do so without charges of trespass. From fall until early spring, the refuge offers Saturday morning island hikes led either by staff or volunteer naturalists. Few local folks seem to be aware of these walks, even though information is posted on the refuge's website. However, members of bird clubs and other outdoor-oriented groups are regulars on the trips, realizing that this is a unique opportunity to visit a wildlife sanctuary rich in both human and natural history.

The Fisherman Island refuge falls under the umbrella of its larger cousin on the mainland, Eastern Shore of Virginia National Wildlife Refuge. The two refuges, along with private conservation ownership and Kiptopeke State Park, protect many acres of critical wildlife habitat on the southern tip of the Delmarva Peninsula. This narrow tip is vital to migrating birds, which stop to replenish fat reserves before crossing eighteen miles of open bay.

The mainland refuge was opened in 1984 on the site of a former military post, which, during World War II, was called Fort John Custis, and later Cape Charles Air

Force Station. The refuge includes maritime forest, shrub thickets, ponds, salt marsh, grassland, and cropland. Hiking trails, a photography blind, and a well-appointed visitor center make the natural history of the area easily accessible to visitors. The refuge also has quite a few remnants of its military history. Huge bunkers were constructed to house sixteen-inch guns to protect Hampton Roads ports, and one such bunker today provides a stunning view of the bay, and, on a clear day, Virginia Beach in the distance. After the war, in 1950, the property was deeded to the Air Force and some of the base housing, offices, and radar units are still there.

Fisherman Island became a wildlife refuge in 1969, although portions of the island at that time remained in private hands. Back then, it was managed as a satellite of Back Bay NWR, but when the Eastern Shore of Virginia NWR was established in 1984 management was transferred there. The entire island today, with the exception of the bridge-tunnel right-of-way, is wildlife refuge, protecting about 1,850 acres of nesting habitat.

Our family tries to get in at least one Fisherman Island hike during the winter. The Saturday hikes begin in October, but we prefer to go in colder weather for a variety of reasons. There usually are dabbling ducks in the shallow ponds and marsh creeks, and the diving ducks are plentiful in the deeper waters. There are also none of the less desirable critters, such as ticks and mosquitoes, which are numerous in warm weather.

With all that in mind, on a winter Saturday, we bundled up and met Jenny and George Budd at the visitor center at Eastern Shore of Virginia National Wildlife Refuge and drove to a small parking area on Fisherman Island. There were about fifteen in our group, led by the Budds, volunteer naturalists who host numerous Fisherman Island trips over the winter. The plan was to hike across the island along an old Navy road, and then walk along the bay to the point where the bridge crosses the island. We then would hike back along the roadway to the parking area.

It wasn't long before we discovered Fisherman's value to migrating wildfowl. A freshwater pond near the center of the island held dozens of ducks. We counted black ducks, widgeon, gadwall, green-winged teal, wood ducks, hooded mergansers, and pied-bill grebes, all on a pond about the size of a football field. As we hiked through the grass along the pond edge, a woodcock flushed from the undergrowth.

"The refuge gets hundreds of woodcock in the winter," said Jenny. "They migrate southward and gather here on the tip of the peninsula before crossing the bay. If we get a prolonged freeze, the birds can suffer because they feed by probing into the soft ground for worms and other prey,"

The freshwater pond is a magnet for wildlife, said Jenny, and it adds greatly to the natural diversity of the island. We found numerous animal tracks along the sandy road that runs along the pond. Deer tracks were everywhere, plus those of raccoon, possibly fox, and river otter. One well-worn path led across a set of low dunes, through a greenbriar thicket, and down to the water.

In the sandy road, we picked up a remnant of last summer. A turtle egg, white and leathery, lay exposed. Inside was a tiny but fully formed turtle, long deceased, its head and shell easily defined. An adult turtle had apparently crawled from the pond to the sandy dune, laid a clutch of eggs, and returned to the water. We found other spent shells without occupants, so perhaps some members of that particular turtle generation survived.

Along the road are not only the remnants of nature, but those of humans. A jumble of steel and concrete are all that remains of a look-out tower, which was dismantled by Navy SEALS some years ago. A concrete bunker/sand dune looks like great bat habitat, and in a clearing on top of it researchers trap and band hawks during the fall migration. Where the road meets the beach, the remains of a large pier mark the last of the military presence on the island, that of the Navy.

According to the Budds, Fisherman Island has had many uses over the years. It was a quarantine station in the late 1800s and early 1900s when there was a cholera epidemic in Europe. Immigrants would be quarantined here before being taken up the bay to Baltimore. It was also used for harbor defense during both World Wars.

The island was privately owned until the 1890s, when the government began condemnation hearings. Plans to turn the island into a wildlife refuge came as early as 1933, when the legislature approved transfer from the War Department to the Department of Agriculture so the island could become a migratory bird refuge. Needs of the military intervened, however, and even in the 1950s the island was being used by the Navy. The Chesapeake Bay Bridge-Tunnel opened in 1964, and five years later the wildlife refuge finally became a reality.

Considering its colorful history, Fisherman is a relatively young island. "A survey in the 1800s showed the island at about twenty-five acres," said George, "but it has grown to 1,850 acres and is apparently still building."

Some accounts indicate that Fisherman was spawned by a shipwreck, when a vessel carrying linen went ashore on a bar at the tip of the peninsula. The linen was salvaged, but the skeleton of the ship remained on the shoal, and sand began to build around it. The resultant island was named Linen Bar by local residents.

"No one really knows whether that story is true," said George, "but it adds a lot to the colorful past of the region. We do know that the island began as a shoal, or group of shoals, and it's still growing. We can't say that about many barrier beaches today."

50

Flatwater Paddling

On Delmarva, A Day Afloat is Close at Hand

One of my favorite Delmarva experiences is simply to spend a day afloat in a small boat. Here on our peninsula, it's not difficult to find a quiet and remote body of water...a place to spend a day, or at least an afternoon, removed from the towns and highways, business and commerce, and just float quietly on flat water, with no itinerary and no schedule to follow.

We have had our share of growth and progress here, but quiet water is still easy to come by, whether you live in Rock Hall or Cape Charles or points in between. Put your canoe in at a public launch facility, and instead of going downstream with the majority of boat traffic, paddle upstream. Follow the blue lines, I say. Look at a local topo map and find a familiar body of water. When the water widens, the blue line becomes a prominent feature of the map. When the waterway narrows, it appears as a narrow blue line, a squiggle disappearing into the green of forest and farm. These blue lines are usually the best places to paddle a canoe or kayak. The water is often narrow, shallow, winding, and unnavigable for motor boats. Perfect for paddling.

Delmarva has hundreds of small creeks that meet this description, and no matter where you live, you can't be far away from one. You can find them in Queen Anne's, or in the marshes of Kent, Talbot, and Dorchester, certainly in Somerset, Wicomico, and Worcester, and on the bayside in Accomack and Northampton. Even our seaside has them, although seaside creeks tend to have a high tidal gradient and swift current, making float trips dependent upon the ebb and flood of tides.

I happen to live on Pungoteague Creek, which is in Accomack County, south of Onancock. It is a rural creek, not far from the bay, with one village and a few farms and residences scattered here and there along its banks. It has many branches, most of which appear on the topo as blue squiggles that dangle like pieces of string off the main stem, threading their way into the upland. If you live in any other county on Delmarva, you could find the equivalent of Pungoteague Creek, which, it seems to me, is one of the wonderful things about our peninsula. We are never far away from a quiet piece of water, and this is something we rarely speak about, but value very highly. I would hate to contemplate life without quiet water being nearby and handy, in case the need arose to be alone and afloat for an afternoon, or maybe more.

There is no feeling quite like sliding a canoe into a flatwater creek, gliding away from shore, feeling for the first time that day the balance of water, the steady fulcrum of the little boat, watching your reflection in black water as if you were floating in space and were weightless. I have no ambition to paddle whitewater, as these streams are noisy and imposing, geology flexing its muscles. Give me the solid black water of the Pocomoke or Nassawango, or my native Pungoteague, pushed and pulled by a gentle tide, a stream whose fingers reach into the mainland through groves of pine woods and thickets of pickerelweed.

This is an essential Delmarva experience, and not necessarily one we can wrap a book chapter around. Paddling flatwater streams does not lend itself to guidebook narrative. It is not a destination as such, no trip to The Green in old Dover to immerse oneself in history. Rather, flatwater paddling is a frame of mind, and you need to find your own stretch of quiet water. The search, of course, is essential to the experience. Read a topo map, launch a boat, and find out what's around the next bend. Call it proactive tourism.

This, perhaps, is the most important aspect of Delmarva, but one too often overlooked. We have history, we have beaches and shopping and bike paths and small towns along back roads. Mostly, though, we have water — quiet, unassuming little creeks and guts that sometimes have no name. Our existence has been tied to these waterways for generations. Our ancestors' lives were tied to the pulse of the tides, the daily push and pull of moon gravity, and this is an important thing to discover.

Our history and culture are immersed in water, as if baptized by nature. We were colonized by Europeans who came by boat. Our foodways are tied to the bays and creeks that surround our peninsula. We favor blue crabs and clam chowder, raw oysters, and rockfish cooked over an open fire. We depend upon the consistency of tides, having faith that they will rise only so far, and then ebb. Perhaps there is an element of spirituality here, an unseen power that manipulates our landscape, feeds us, gives us places to float alone on quiet water, to learn our landscape, and know ourselves. This, it seems to me, is the essence of our peninsula, the ultimate Delmarva experience.

Index of Places